From Olympus to Camelot

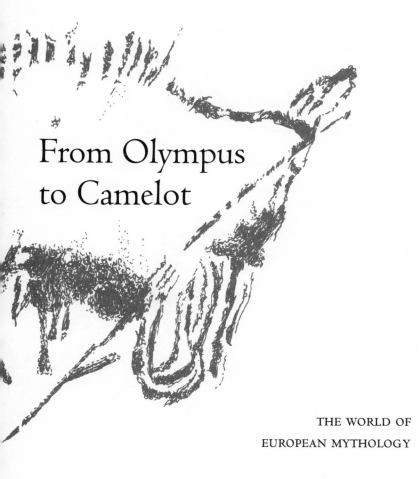

From Olympus
to Camelot

THE WORLD OF
EUROPEAN MYTHOLOGY

David Leeming

OXFORD
UNIVERSITY PRESS
2003

OXFORD
UNIVERSITY PRESS

Oxford New York

Auckland Bangkok Buenos Aires Cape Town Chennai
Dar es Salaam Delhi Hong Kong Istanbul Karachi Kolkata
Kuala Lumpur Madrid Melbourne Mexico City Mumbai Nairobi
São Paulo Shanghai Taipei Tokyo Toronto

Published by Oxford University Press, Inc.
198 Madison Avenue, New York, New York, 10016
www.oup.com

Oxford is a registered trademark of Oxford University Press

Library of Congress Cataloging-in-Publication Data
Leeming, David Adams, 1937–
From Olympus to Camelot: the world of European mythology / David Leeming.
p. cm.
Includes bibliographical references and index.
ISBN 0-19-514361-2
1. Mythology, European.
I. Title.
BL689 .L44 2003
291.1'3'094—dc21
2002011740

Book design and composition by Susan Day

1 3 5 7 9 10 8 6 4 2
Printed in the United States of America
on acid-free paper

Preface

THIS BOOK WILL treat the great mythological traditions of the European continent in a historical, cultural, and comparative context. The subject has particular appeal not only because of the tumultuous history of European tribal warfare which continues to this day, but because of the current attempt of many Europeans to see themselves as a single—albeit multicultural—entity. There are, of course, built-in limitations when a study is restricted by borders that are the result of wars, arbitrary assignment, or even geographical factors such as rivers or mountains. Although there are sometimes clear geographic reasons for the concept of nations and continents, myths do not necessarily recognize such reasons. When we speak of European, Asian, African, or Middle Eastern mythology, we are to some extent simply taking advantage of a convenient but, from the mythological perspective, arbitrary arrangement provided for us. This is especially so when we consider the possible nature of the myths of early *Homo sapiens*, for whom Ice Age life in what is now northern Germany, for example, would in all likelihood not have differed significantly from life at the same time in what is now Iraq. And while it is possible to see certain patterns in Asian or Middle

Eastern mythology, for instance, it is just as easy to find connections between myths of the land we now call India and those we
now call Ireland or Germany or Greece.

Still, given the geopolitical existence of Europe, particularly as
a modern concept, it makes sense to study the myths that have
found their way to the continent over the centuries and have quite
obviously affected the lifestyles and actions of the peoples who
have settled there. To understand what it is to be European, it is
helpful to examine the cultural dreams of the people who have
settled in Europe.

My approach takes us first to a definition of terms, beginning
with "myth" itself, and to a historical overview of cultural development on the continent from the time of so-called Neanderthal
man to the more recognizable, predominantly Indo-European
cultures, such as the various expressions of what we now call the
Germanic, Celtic, Baltic, Slavic, Greek, and Roman.

The first myths, those of the Paleolithic and early Neolithic
periods are, in the absence of written evidence, locked in mystery
and can only be approached in a suppositional manner by way of
archeology and comparison with later cultural expressions.
Turning to the high Neolithic era and the development of Indo-
European myth, we can be more specific. And as we move into
later periods, we are on still more familiar ground, even as we remember that myths are often, in part, the inventions of story-
tellers whose individual and cultural priorities color the great
sagas that are their storytelling vehicles.

Although this is not a comprehensive handbook of all the
myths of Europe, central to the book are specific European
myths—some familiar, some not so familiar—that I have
treated first in relation to particular cultures and then in a comparative context as examples of creation stories, deity types, and
heroes. The assumption here is that there are significant differences between the mythologies of various cultural groups, but
that something approximating a European mythology emerges

from the substructure of those different understandings, most noticeably when the mythology associated with Christianity becomes prominent.

My assumption is that the reader who examines all of the myths contained here will have experienced a significant element of the European psyche and the mythological process by which it has developed into its present form.

Contents

Myths and Mythologies

THE WORD "MYTH" has had many—often conflicting—meanings attached to it, all of which have some validity. On the level of everyday usage a myth is a false story or belief. The common meaning applies in some sense to hallowed religious stories as well. For most people it is a myth that walking under a ladder brings bad luck. But it is also fair to say that for a non-Jew and probably for many practicing Jews, the parting of the Red Sea is a myth, or that for non-Christians and many Christians, the Resurrection is a myth. In this sense a myth is a story that is outside the scope of our actual experience and therefore, literally, impossible or false. Seas do not part and humans are not resurrected. The Red Sea myth and the Resurrection myth, however, are very different from the under the ladder myth because, for the cultures to which they belong, they convey some significant truth about the relationship between human beings and the source of being.

Myth has always had an explanatory or etiological aspect. Myths have traditionally explained such phenomena as death, the changing of seasons, the passage of the sun and the moon, and the origin of the universe and life itself. Myths have served, too, as the basis for rituals intending to preserve a proper relationship between humanity and the mysterious unknown. For the anthropologist or sociologist, myths reveal the nature of cultures.

For many psychologists and modern mythologists, myths reveal the inner workings of the human psyche. These thinkers note that when we compare myths from around the world, we discover that many cultures have, for instance, resurrection myths, virgin birth myths, dying god myths, or myths of the hero descending into the underworld. Carl Jung, Mircea Eliade, Joseph Campbell, and many others have emphasized this archetypal or universal aspect of myth. For these universalist mythologists, myths are at once cultural and universal collective dreams that can tell us much about not only who and what cultures are but who and what we are as a species.

According to the universalist approach, myths might be called the most basic expressions of a defining aspect of the human species—the need and ability to understand and to tell stories to reflect our understanding, whether or not we know the real facts. Humans, unlike other animals, are blessed or cursed with consciousness and specifically with the consciousness of plot—of beginnings, middles, and ends. We wonder individually, culturally, and as a species about our origins, about the significance of our present time, and we think continually of the future. We are always aware of the journey aspect of our existence. So it has always been that adults have told stories to children to describe our journey, and leaders have told their people stories for the same reason.

Inevitably, what begins as metaphor grows for some into divine word that is literal and absolute truth. Just as inevitably, many humans have insisted on confusing the logic of history and science with the quite different logic that is mytho-logic or mythology. In terms of history, the myths of Thor's hammer, or the travels of Gilgamesh, or the parting of the Red Sea are, to say the least, questionable as literal truth, but when we think of these stories mythologically, they take on an importance, a truth, without which we would lose our very identity as cultures and as humans. Thor's hammer conveys a Scandinavian and ultimately a human sense of a terrible and wonderful power of fertility in the universe that is difficult to explain in any historical or scientific sense. The travels of Gilgamesh express the ancient Sumerian-Babylonian search for meaning, a search that metaphorically is still very much ours. The parting of the Red Sea speaks to the sense that a culture (but also humanity itself) is somehow unique and special and that humans do best when they make proper use of that uniqueness in relation to the larger mysteries of the universe.

Myths, then, may be thought of as universal metaphors or dreams, what mythologist William Doty calls "projective psyche models" (Doty, xviii). But it must be emphasized that myths require cultural clothes to take on life, to become concrete. Any given cultural clothes are usually insufficient, however, to convey completely and ultimately such archetypal concepts as Supreme Deity, Creation, and the Hero Journey. By taking into consideration the metaphors and dreams of all cultures we come closer to a sense of the real nature and significance of those concepts. To put this another way, Slavic myths will tell us a great deal about the priorities and characteristics of the Slavic people but will present a limited picture of the concept of the goddess, for example. But when we compare the goddess myths of the Indo-European cultures and, in the case of this book, the cultures of Europe, we gain a clearer vision of the Indo-European or European goddess and of the Indo-European or European psyche or soul. Once again it is useful, then, to think of myths as cultural and universal human dreams. By studying the many myth-dreams of Europe culturally and then comparatively, we hope to better understand the cultures of Europe and Europe as a collective entity.

PART I

The Background

I

The Mythology
of Prehistoric Europe

IT IS IMPOSSIBLE to be precise about the origins of mythology in Europe or anywhere else. The emergence of a tool-making protohuman being, *Homo habilis*, occurred some 2.2 to 1.6 million years ago in East Africa, and was followed by the more advanced *Homo erectus*, of whom remains dating from about 750,000 B.C.E. have been found in the European continent. It is not until the middle of the Paleolithic or Stone Age, the period marked by the development of stone tools that coincides with the geologic and climatological Pleistocene or Ice Age—that is, sometime after 500,000 and before 200,000 B.C.E.—that we find in the Europe of the so-called Heidelberg man (named for the skeletal remains of a *Homo erectus* found near Heidelberg, Germany, in 1907) the first tenuous archeological hints of what might possibly have been mythological conceptualization. It was then that symmetrical tools were crafted in sizes large enough to suggest ritual use, which prompted mythologist Joseph Campbell to hypothesize a "mythology and ritual lore of the hand ax, which in later myth and cult became linked to the idea of thunder (Thor's hammer, the bolt of Zeus, Indra, etc.)" (*Primitive*, 393). From the same period are crudely formed triangular stone figures that Marija

Gimbutas associates with an early stage of goddess mythology (*Language*, 237).

At the center of any mythology, of course, is story, and we cannot be certain of the details of a story without the connecting link of written or spoken language. Until the development of writing, we are denied linguistic access to any mythology and must depend on such physical evidence of story as exists in burial grounds, rock carvings, cave paintings, and small artifacts. It is also possible to hypothesize the nature of the myths of preliterate periods by studying myths and rituals of peoples who continue "primitive" practices in the modern era—such examination being prompted by obvious common themes such as the sacrifice of a maiden or the presence of a serpent in a tree (see, e.g., Campbell, *Primitive*, ch. 6).

The Middle Paleolithic

We can probably assume that in Europe, as in other parts of the world, mythology first took form when humans evolved to the point where their inherent mimetic abilities—their tendency to make believe—were applied to a social, even cosmic, rather than merely individual sense of identity. Archeology suggests that proto-Paleolithic and Paleolithic humans in Europe and elsewhere created a body of symbols that formed the basis for what eventually became myths, stories with beginnings, middles, and ends—the essential elements of the Aristotelian plot or *mythos*—that were in all likelihood related to ritual and that expressed a sense of the nature of existence and the human place in it. The existence of such a symbolic language in a developed system of myth and ritual is strongly suggested, for instance, in connection with *Homo sapiens neanderthalensis* or *Homo neanderthalensis* (Neanderthal man), a distant predecessor or sub-species of our own species, *Homo sapiens*. Neanderthal refers to the Neander Valley in Germany, where skeletal remains were discovered in the mid-nineteenth century. Other Neanderthal sites have since been found in the Middle East and especially in other parts of Europe, where *Homo neanderthalensis* represented the human species from about 250,000 B.C.E. to about 40,000 B.C.E.

Recent studies present a different view of this predecessor of our form of the species than the apelike unintelligent, cannibal, club-wielding, woman-dragging cave man image with which we are all familiar. That the species was unintelligent or merely apelike is belied by the existence of a surprisingly large brain cavity and by indications of a mythological consciousness. The primary evidence for such a consciousness—specifically for the belief in a metaphysical realm—lies in the strange and seemingly impractical but carefully arranged collections of objects in middle Paleolithic Neanderthal burial sites in Europe and elsewhere.

In excavations in the village of Le Moustier and the nearby villages of La Chapelle-aux-Saints and La Ferrassie in southwest France, for instance, whole skeletons or separated skulls have been found surrounded or covered by valuable objects such as bits of quartz and jasper, bone plates, and tools—perhaps supplies for survival in another world. The soil seems to have been colored by red ocher, suggesting a ceremonial approach to death. Some bodies appear to have been buried in fetal or sleeping positions, possibly indicating that death was seen as a sleeping period that might lead to new birth. Many scholars have suggested that these and other Neanderthal sites in Europe—and in Israel and Iraq as well—suggest an early myth of the afterlife (see, e.g., Narr, 151ff; Campbell, *Animal Powers*, 51ff).

Joseph Campbell sees still more indication of Neanderthal's mythological character in the discovery of bear sanctuaries in caves of the high Alps (*Primitive*, 339ff). In such caves, bear skulls are set into "altar" niches, suggesting a worshiping of animal spirits and an early belief in the willing participation of animals in the life-giving process of killing and eating. Although the hunt itself was a source of survival for these hunter-gatherers,

the special treatment of animal bones and dead human bodies
was not. The practice may reasonably be attributed to the pecu-
liarly human realm of *mytho*-logic. Campbell sees the Neanderthal bear sanctuaries as the "earliest evidence anywhere on
earth of the veneration of a divine being" and as an indication
of ritual sacrifice (*Animal Powers*, 147). For Campbell the bear
sanctuaries were the source for bear cults that would spread
across northern Europe and Asia into North America. In connection with these cults, particularly in light of the fact that hi-
bernation was a mystery for early humans—one augmented by
the ability of the bear to stand and even walk upright like
them—the question arises whether this bear "god" was the first
of many who seemed to die only to return later to life, who, if
treated properly in a ritual context, would allow himself to be
killed for the good of all?

The modern existence of bear ceremonies and stories—
especially among the Ainu of Japan and several Native American groups—possibly can give us at least a partial sense of
the nature of the early bear cult and its myths. Among the
Ainu, a black bear raised from an early age in a cage is sacrificed, and its pelt is ritually served a stew made of its own
flesh. Cherokee Indians told James Mooney in the late nineteenth century the story of a young man who was adopted by
a bear after the bear proved magically invincible before his arrows (Leeming, *Voyage*, 229–31). When a year had passed and
the man had grown bearlike fur, the host informed him that
the Indians would return and would succeed in killing him,
but that if the "bear man" followed certain instructions, all
would be well. When the hunters arrived, they killed the bear
and discovered their long lost—now furry—cohort in the
cave. After skinning the bear, the hunters watched as the bear
man—now a de facto bear shaman or medicine man—performed the ritual over the bear's remains. As the men left,
they looked back to see the bear rising from the bones.

The Upper Paleolithic

Neanderthal humans were replaced and/or absorbed by about 40,000 B.C.E. by a *Homo sapiens* subspecies anatomically almost identical to modern human beings. Recent discoveries suggest this subspecies emerged in Africa as early as 130,000 years ago. The European remains of our immediate ancestors were unearthed in the late 1860s in the Dordogne region of France. This stage of *Homo sapiens* has sometimes also been referred to as Cro-Magnon man after a place in which the archeological remains were particularly rich. Cro-Magnon man, like his significantly shorter Neanderthal predecessor, possessed a cranial capacity at least as large as that of today's humans and was a hunter-gatherer highly adept in tool invention and artistry. We know Cro-Magnon best from the rock carvings, burial grounds, and figurines from regions that span modern-day France, Germany, and parts of eastern Europe, and especially from the painted caves of France and northern Spain.

Most scholars believe that *Homo sapiens* of the upper Paleolithic in Europe had developed religious systems. Karl Narr believes that a grave in Brno in the Czech Republic, containing ocher, carefully cut fossil ornaments, stone rings, and stone, bone, and ivory disks, as well as a small male figurine, suggests the burial of a cultic figure and some sort of elaborate ceremonial practice (Narr, 154ff). Although they disagree on specific interpretation, Narr, Joseph Campbell, André Leroi-Gourhan, Abbé Henri Breuil, and later scholars of Paleolithic art believe that ritual and associated mythology are especially indicated by the great paintings of the "cave temples" such as Les Trois Frères and Lascaux (see Narr, 155ff; Campbell, *Primitive*, 374ff; Campbell, *Animal Powers*, 58ff). And the existence of large numbers of rock carvings and small figurines depicting females with exaggerated breasts, buttocks, and stomachs, as well as stylized impressions of the vulva on these figures and in isolation, all suggest to

Marija Gimbutas and her many followers the existence in the upper Paleolithic of a goddess-based religion.

It is only possible, of course, to surmise the nature of the mythology associated with these various remnants of the Paleolithic. Clearly it is the caves and the female figurines that call for the most attention.

Beginning with the caves, we are inevitably struck by the dominance in the paintings of animals on the one hand, and of beings who appear to be part animal and part human or, more likely, humans masked or disguised as animals on the other. This animalist focus is not surprising for a hunting society. What is of particular interest is the impression given in the cave paintings of a ceremonial dance of sorts involving the hunters and the hunted, humans and animals. That is, we seem almost certainly to be in the presence of a ritual process through which the animal agrees to be sacrificed. Depictions of wounded bison and bear

Rock painting of the sorcerer, a shaman-trickster god.
Les Trois Frères Cave, France; ca. 14,000 B.C.E.
Drawing by Jake Page, after Ablé H. Breuil.

The bear of Les Trois Frères. Drawing by Jake Page.

are found in the caves, as might be expected. Perhaps the most famous wounded animal is the great blood-spouting bear of Les
Trois Frères, but this bear stands beneath the even more famous
antlered dancing shaman or sorcerer.

The importance of the bear—a descendant perhaps of our Neanderthal bear god—is further suggested by a model of a large bear
in a cavern at Montespan in front of which was found a bear's skull
covered by the remains of a bear's pelt. It is difficult not to agree
with Campbell's assessment that a bear ceremonial and mythology
are indicated in this altar arrangement. The bear, a kind of totem
spirit or animal master, seems likely to have been the object of a
"sacramental hunt," the center of what Campbell describes as "the
mythology of the Great Hunt in perfect flower" (*Primitive*, 378).

Anyone who has been present at an animal dance performed
during ceremonies at the Indian pueblos of the American southwest will find many of the paintings in the cave temples strangely
familiar. A visitor to the San Felipe Pueblo in New Mexico (between Santa Fe and Albuquerque) attending a ceremony ostensibly
in celebration of the Christian Feast of Candlemas or Candelaria
(the purification of the Virgin Mary or the presentation of Christ
at the Temple), for example, will see what is in effect a mystery
play of the willing sacrifice of animals, which gives the impression of having emerged from some ancient practice closer to the
cave paintings than to the rituals of the Christian church. (There

Pueblo Indian masked dancer.
Drawing by Jake Page.

Masked dancer of Les Trois Frères.
Drawing by Jake Page.

is, of course, a *mythological* connection between the sacrificed buffalo king of San Felipe and the crucified Christ and between the maiden who dances with the buffalo and the Virgin Mary, who accepts her role as the human vessel for the divine seed.) Here, as at all the other pueblos in the area—at Christmas time or other religious holidays and pueblo feast days— men wearing great antlers or buffalo masks dance in the village square, impersonating the animals of the hunt, accompanied by medicine men and other members of the given tribe. They carry sticks that sometimes appear to represent phalluses but more often are used as forelegs on which they lean forward as they and their fellow dancers move their feet in steps eerily reminiscent of the famous, sometimes ithyphallic masked dancers depicted at least 15,000 years ago in Les Trois Frères. The viewer will inevitably be moved by the dance of a village maiden with the buffalo king, by the sacrifice of the animals one by one as the ceremony progresses, and by the return of the animals later in the day.

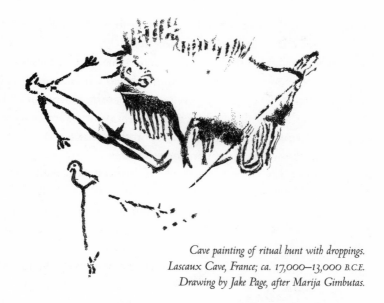

Cave painting of ritual hunt with droppings.
Lascaux Cave, France; ca. 17,000–13,000 B.C.E.
Drawing by Jake Page, after Marija Gimbutas.

Leroi-Gourhon and Campbell find in a repeated pattern in the Paleolithic caves a clue to what they see as an "essential legend of the period," a legend particularly evident in the much-discussed depiction in Lascaux of an ithyphallic, bird-headed man lying prostrate between a bird-headed stick and a large bison that has been penetrated through its anus by a spear, causing its guts to hang basketlike from its abdomen (Campbell, *Animal Powers*, 65–6).

It is, of course, impossible to know what this legend might be, any more than we can know for sure the actual myth behind the dances of the secretive clans of the modern Pueblo Indians, but Campbell calls the Lascaux painting "our first known (yet unknown) mythology, having flourished, one way or another, from c. 17,000 to 12,000 B.C.E. ... very probably the inspiring legend of the entire grotto ..." (*Powers*, 155).

Turning to the female figurines and rock carvings, we find still more mystery but a strong aura of mythology. It should be pointed out that generally the female depictions occur in areas meant for dwelling, whereas the ritual hunting scenes are under the earth, available only to those who venture there for ritual purposes. Once again, a visitor to a southwestern pueblo will notice a striking similarity. Underground places called kivas are restricted places where primarily men perform secret ritual ceremonies associated with the given clan's totem animal. Kivas contain altars and various ritual objects and are themselves representative of the inner earth, the womb of the Great Mother out of whom the people once emerged. Dwelling places, on the other hand, are the precinct of the women, who, in societies that are frequently matrilineal, often own the houses in which they live with their families. For the Pueblo Indians as for the ancient people of the Paleolithic, women's mysteries—her cycles, apparently associated with those of the moon, her birth-giving powers—are an important source of mythology.

Venus of Laussel. Drawing by Jake Page.

The best known of the European rock carvings of a female figure is the so-called Venus of Laussel, a tiny (17-cm or 7-inch) image dating from about 20,000 B.C.E. that was discovered in 1911 on a ledge wall under a limestone overhang sheltering the ruins of a Paleolithic dwelling site near Lascaux. The Venus is one of many images found under the Laussel overhang, all of which point to a mythology of female mysteries and, perhaps, of the moon—a mythology based on such phenomena as menstruation, pregnancy, lactation, and, of course, birth. The Venus herself stands naked, her great maternal breasts reaching almost to a pronounced belly on which her left hand rests, calling attention to the navel and pubic triangle below. Meanwhile her right hand holds up what appears to be a symbolic object—an animal horn or, some have suggested, a crescent moon. "In a posture and with a gesture eloquent of some legend, the knowledge of which has been lost," writes Joseph Campbell, "the Venus of Laussel stands before us like the figment of a dream, of which we dimly know but cannot bring to mind the meaning. The mythology of which she is the messenger remains in absolute silence behind her, like the rock out of which she is hewn" (*Animal Powers*, 66).

That the mythology of the Venus of Laussel has to do with the generative mystery of female-ness, as suggested by Marija Gimbutas and others, is further indicated by the profusion of tiny upper Paleolithic female figurines discovered throughout most of the European continent. Made of stone, bones, and antlers, these figurines greatly outnumber male images. A Venus in Moravia con-tains holes in its head that Camp-bell thinks may have been put there to hold plants and feathers relating to ceremonies of fertility and growth (*Animal Powers*, 70). The Venus of Lespugne in the Pyrenees is a highly stylized, al-most abstract celebration of the elements of the procreative fe-male. The most famous of the figurines is the Venus of Willen-dorf in Austria, who, with her huge breasts, buttocks, and belly, has become the symbol for many of the collective ancestor of the gradually more individualized Neolithic great goddess.

Venus of Willendorf. Drawing by Jake Page.

Venus of Lespugne. Drawing by Jake Page.

The Neolithic and Copper Age: Old Europe

In the Neolithic (ca. 10,000 B.C.E.–ca. 3000 B.C.E.), the period
coinciding with the development of what are essentially the cli-
matic conditions of our era, humans continued to hunt and to
gather but turned increasingly to agriculture as a means of sub-
sistence. With agriculture came permanent community living
places, the domestication of animals, the development of pottery, and, one assumes, more organized religious and mythological systems—including what Dragoslav Srejovic calls "the de-
sacralization of stone," stone having been the central element
of the Paleolithic, and "the sacralization of earth," the essential element of the Neolithic (Srejovic, 352). Given the reasonably obvious analogy between the seemingly miraculous procreative aspect of females and the equally mysterious process by
which earth receives seeds and produces crops, it is hardly surprising that people of the Neolithic would have built on the
symbolism already present in the Paleolithic, as, for instance, in
the stone Venuses of Laussel and Willendorf, and would have
developed a mythology of the earth as mother goddess. We can
safely assume, at least, that the awe and wonder we associate
with religion would have been related to the birth-giving aspect
of earth as a mother and eventually on the male as a seed or
seed-bearer as well, and that myths would have formed around
these figures and their activities. Such a mythology is evident
enough in the much-discussed Neolithic ruins of the Fertile
Crescent of the Near East, with their images of enthroned and
birth-giving goddesses and bull gods. The evidence is just as
clear in Neolithic Europe. Leaving aside such disputed subjects
as the valuation applied to male as opposed to female figures in
Neolithic mythology and the question as to whether goddess
religions imply matriarchal cultures, it is clear enough from
archeological evidence that goddess religions, and probably
mythologies, were in full flower in what Marija Gimbutas calls

"Old Europe," at least from the seventh millennium B.C.E. Old Europe refers to the period before the dominance of the Indo-European invaders who came down into Europe from the Eurasian steppes between ca. 4500 and 2500 B.C.E. Gimbutas makes a strong case for goddess-based, gynocentric religion and mythology in Old Europe until its gradual displacement by the patriarchal structures of the warlike invaders ("Prehistoric Religions: Old Europe," 11:506ff). The Old European religion according to this theory was maintained in parts of continental Europe until as late as 2000 B.C.E. and in the somewhat isolated islands of the Aegean and Mediterranean, most notably in Crete, until at least 1500 B.C.E. Gimbutas argues that in spite of the official disintegration of the Old European religion and its replacement by male-dominated pantheons, the old traditions "formed a powerful substratum that profoundly affected the religious life of European cultures that arose in the Bronze Age" and later—cultures that preserved the earth mother and her mysteries in figures such as Gaia, in earth-based rites and mythologies such as that of Demeter at Eleusis, in the tradition of earth-centered Irish queens such as Maeve, and much later in the development of the cult of the Virgin Mary (11:506).

Naturally, the development of many cultural groups in Old Europe would have resulted in a variety of specific beliefs and traditions, but archeological evidence supports the theory that a de facto universal European religion during the period in question was dominated by a great mother and related issues of planting, birth-giving, feminine and lunar cycles, and what Gimbutas calls the "awe and mystery surrounding the cyclic destruction and regeneration of life" (11:507).

The archeological record of the goddess religion and mythology in Europe is extensive. Gimbutas isolates several figures from this record. There is, for instance, what Gimbutas calls a "Bird-Goddess" from Thessaly, dating from the sixth millennium B.C.E., complete with beak, wings, and large buttocks.

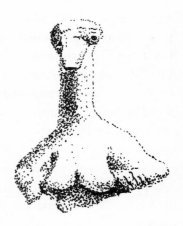

Bird Goddess. Drawing by Jake Page.

A snake goddess also appears in the early Vinca culture near Belgrade as well as in other areas. The snake goddess often has horns which, for Gimbutas, link her to the crescent moon and lunar cycles and suggest her kinship with earlier Paleolithic Venuses as, perhaps, house shrines used to promote general welfare (11:507). The bird and snake goddess figures, whether depicted as separate entities or as one being, are associated with life-giving water and air. The zigzag meandering designs signifying the snake goddess in early Vinca artifacts are similar to

The snake goddess. Clay figurine, burnished dark gray and encrusted with white lines. Kato Lerapetra, S. Crete; ca. 6000–5500 B.C.E. Drawing by Jake Page.

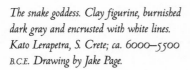

designs also signifying water on North American Indian pottery, designs related to a mythology that ties the serpent figure
not only to the lightning of the sky but to the rivers with
sources deep within the earth.

Particularly vivid depictions of what must have been a Neolithic bird/snake goddess mythology are found in Crete. This
figure above, dating from ca. 6000 B.C.E. has a birdlike face and a
snakelike lower body. She is perhaps the ancestor of those later
Minoan goddess-priestesses with exposed breasts proudly holding snakes aloft.

It is tempting to wonder whether the story of Eve and the
serpent is not somehow a distortion of an earlier, more compat-
ible relationship between a goddess and her serpent companion,
a companion who brings the
knowledge of the underearth to
the world above.

Among the most clearly mythological of archeological goddess
discoveries is that of the "white
lady" or "death goddess," the
ancestor of goddesses in India
and elsewhere, who in death take
the living back to earth as part of
the regenerative process of life.
This death-wielding aspect is, of
course, reflected in the lunar cycles or rising and dying, waxing
and waning, by which goddesses
have generally been symbolized.

The stiff nude, or the white lady (Death).
Clay figurine from a young girl's grave;
late Cucuteni culture. Vykhvatintsi cemetery,
Moldavia; ca. 3500 B.C.E. Drawing by Jake Page.

The death goddess is sometimes depicted as a nude lying stiffly with legs closed and arms close to the sides as if laid out for burial, but with a clearly defined and stylized triangular pubic area signifying, as always, the life that will follow death.

Early Bronze Age from Poliochni, Lemnos;
ca. 3000–2500 B.C.E. Drawing by Jake Page.

Sometimes the death goddess takes the form of that ancient harbinger of death, the mysterious owl. This burial urn, dating from ca. 3000 B.C.E. on Lemnos, is clearly an owl goddess complete with breasts, navel and, most importantly, a prominent vulva through which, possibly, the dead may be reborn.

The best known of the Neolithic goddess depictions are perhaps the enthroned pregnant figures of such places as Çatal Hüyük and Hacilar in Anatolia.

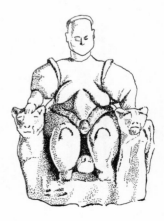

The goddess of Çatal Hüyük giving birth.
Anatolia; ca. 6000 B.C.E. Drawing by Jake
Page, after James Mellaart.

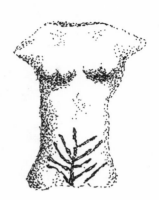

Goddess of Regeneration. Drawing by Jake Page.

Goddesses of regeneration and procreation are also ubiquitous in Neolithic Europe. This sixth millennium B.C.E. Vincan
figurine represents the ancestor of the grain mother, the fertility
goddess found in most parts of the later Neolithic world. Here,
sprouting plants emerge from her vulva.

This version of the great birth-giver was found in Malta and
dates from the fourth millennium B.C.E. Pregnancy is evident, and
the prominence of the birth passage is emphasized by means of
exaggerated size and the position of the right arm. The stripes
on the back signify the nine months of gestation.

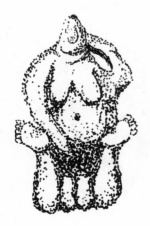

*Birth-giving Goddess.
Drawing by Jake Page.*

Ca. 4th mill. B.C.E. Goddess temple of the giant of Cuzo in Malta.
Drawing by Jake Page, after Rob Wood.

The great goddess of the Neolithic in Europe was also represented in the megalithic ("great stone") temple architecture found
in many parts of Europe, including Spain, Germany, Sweden,
France, and Britain. Marija Gimbutas takes issue with those scholars
who speak of a separate megalithic culture and megalithic religion

Goddess tomb. Shanballyemond,
Ireland; ca. 4th mill. B.C.E.
Drawing by Jake Page.

Goddess tombs Gloucestershire, England
ca. 3000 B.C.E. Drawing by Jake Page.

associated with such great megaliths as Stonehenge ("Megalithic Religion," 9:337). For her, the stone circles, Maltese temples, burial chambers, and great standing stones or menhirs of Brittany and the British isles are all local expressions of the gynocentric mythology that she sees as pervasive on the European continent from the upper Paleolithic well into the Neolithic. The temples and tombs, she believes, stand for the pregnant earth goddess or the death goddess, as suggested by this drawing of the stone temple of Malta.

In Ireland too are found anthropomorphic architecture suggesting the goddess in the so-called court tombs, where the center of the structure is the uterus, again suggesting a myth of rebirth.

And there are vaginalike entrances to the long barrows of Neolithic Britain, indicating the same mythology.

This is not to say that no male deities existed during the period of goddess dominance or that only gynocentric issues were present in myth and religion. Not surprisingly, we find frequent images of an ithyphallic descendant of the upper Paleolithic

Ithyphallic figure of a year god with right hand at the cheek and left hand holding phallus; Dimini culture. Found near Larisa, Greece; first half of fifth millennium B.C.E. Drawing by Jake Page.

shaman-animal master, an appropriate companion to a goddess whose primary characteristic is fertility. Sometimes these are young and ithyphallic, perhaps suggesting the renewal of life; sometimes they are clearly sad and old, indicating the death of the year or the end of life. They are usually referred to as Year Spirits or Year Gods.

Enthroned vegetation god. Sesklo, Pyrasos near Volos, Thessaly; ca. 5900–5700 B.C.E. Drawing by Jake Page.

In the combination of these gods and goddesses of the early Neolithic, we are very likely in the presence of an emerging seasonally based mythology of sacrifice, death, and renewal related to the development of the sedentary, agricultural cultures beginning in the eighth millennium B.C.E.—a mythology that was to take many forms, including, as in the Near East, a cult of a sacrificial bull god, and culminating in the central myth of Christianity in the common era. Other mythological themes are indicated by Neolithic sites, especially those in southeastern Europe. Dragoslav Srejovic argues that the north-west arrangements of altars in relation to the east-west arrangements of bodies in burial shrines in the Danube region probably represent the division of the world in a creation myth. In the intertwining of male and female signs in proximity to open hearths he sees the theme of fertilization and a "cult of the domestic hearth" (Srejovic, 356–7).

Again, it must be emphasized that in the absence of written record we can only hypothesize as to the myths of the Paleolithic and early Neolithic in Europe. A comparison with later cultures that possess similar symbols can be helpful, but the only statement that can be made with some confidence is that archeological evidence points to the clear existence of mythic figures and mythic narratives in Old Europe.

To understand something of what these figures and their stories might have looked like, we can consider the vegetation-fertility myths of Mesopotamia, where writing was developed by about 3500 B.C.E. and at least fragments of an ancient Sumerian mythology were captured for later study. Central to this mythology are the figures of the goddess Inanna, who descends to the underworld and is revived, and her lover (perhaps brother) Dumuzi, who is chosen to take her place in the underworld for part of each year as a kind of ransom-seed for Inanna's revival. It is somehow eerie to finally have contact through words with a previously voiceless mythology of sacrifice, fertility, and renewal that is suggested by cave paintings, burial sites, and figurines. This is the earth goddess speaking in her Sumerian form as Inanna. One can suppose that her European equivalents spoke in a similar way:

> He shaped my loins with his fair hands,
> The shepherd Dumuzi filled my lap with cream and milk,
> ...
> He watered my womb (Leeming and Page, *God*, 80).

2

The Indo-Europeans

A Common Mythology?

B Y THE MIDDLE of the sixth millennium B.C.E. European peoples, especially in the more temperate southeast region, had become established villagers, skilled both in agriculture and the domestication of animals. Their pottery, copper, bone, and stone work had developed considerably, and they had learned to use sailing craft for trade. In fact, the southern European cultures were well on their way to becoming what the great city cultures of the Near East and Crete would become in the third and second millennia. But beginning in the late fourth millennium or early third millennium B.C.E. Europe was gradually overrun and radically changed by people from the north, who also made their way into India and Iran to the east and eventually to Crete. By the end of the second millennium, all of Europe, much of Anatolia, the Fertile Crescent, Iran, and much of India were dominated by people most of whom we now refer to collectively as Indo-Europeans—or, in the case of the Fertile Crescent, Semites, who possessed qualities similar to the Indo-Europeans and who had replaced older cultures such as the Sumerian (see Mallory, 149–50). These peoples are the direct mythic and linguistic ancestors of much of the modern world, including Europeans, with the exception of the Turks, the Basques, and peoples whose language stems from the Finno-Ugric (Uralic) family—that is, the Finns, Hungarians, and Estonians. Not only the Indic and Iranian languages, but the Greek, Italic, Celtic, Germanic, Baltic, and Slavic groups are all offshoots of a proto-Indo-European language. It is only natural that we should wonder who these Indo-Europeans were.

The assumption of a proto-Indo-European culture and language out of which the Indo-European invaders sprang is based primarily on linguistic, mythological, ritualistic, and archeological correspondences. It was James Parson in his *The Remains of Japhet* (1767) who noted patterns such as the similar words for numbers in Irish, Welsh, Greek, Latin, and other European languages. Sir William "Oriental" Jones, a more reputable scholar, expanded the patterns in the late eighteenth century to include Sanskrit (the ancient language of India) and Persian. Jones's position is supported by the existence of similar words for such common concepts as deity—e.g., *deus* in Latin, *dios* in Greek, *devha* in Sanskrit, and *daeva* in Persian. Nineteenth century scholars—Rasmus Rusk, August Schleicher, Johannes Schmidt, Jacob Grimm, and others—contributed to the Indo-European hypothesis based on linguistic studies. Karl Müller, F. Max Muller, George W. Cox, and more recently, Georges Dumézil, J. P. Mallory, Jaan Puhvel, and Bruce Lincoln have concentrated more on mythological patterns as well as on linguistic issues (see Eliade, *Encyclopedia*, 7:198–213; and Mallory, ch. 1).

To better understand the sources of the mythological patterns, it is important to consider what little we know—primarily by way of archeology—of these early invaders from the north. There are many theories about the proto-Indo-Europeans. In one of the most popular theories, Marija Gimbutas refers to them as people of the "Kurgan Culture" (*Language*, xx). These were people of the Russian steppes who buried their important male dead in chambers in underground barrows, the Russian word for which is *kurgan.* The archeology of the burial sites and the evidence of language and myth in later Indo-European cultures suggests that these proto-Indo-Europeans were patriarchal and patrilineal, warlike, seminomadic pastoralists who practiced cattle herding, some small scale agriculture, and animal husbandry, and who at least by the sixth millennium B.C.E. had domesticated the horse and trained it to pull wheeled vehicles such as chariots. The Kurgans possessed sophisticated weaponry, including the bow and arrow and metal knives and spears. Given the weaponry, the horse and chariot, and the herds which were apparently the primary measure of wealth, it is not surprising that military raids involving the stealing of cattle were an important activity for these peoples. A much later equivalent would be the raiding in the fifteenth century by the newly arrived seminomadic, pastoralist Athabascan (Navajo and Apache) peoples of the sedentary Pueblo people in the American southwest.

Wherever the Indo-Europeans originated, it is clear that they brought certain mythological themes with them when they migrated south. These themes would take specific form in the mythological traditions we associate now with societies as widely diverse as those, for instance, of India, Greece, Iceland, and Ireland, with religious systems as various as Hinduism and Christianity.

The first of these themes has been called tripartization. Early in the twentieth century, sociologist Emile Durkheim postulated that myths reflected a given culture's social arrangements. Greek and Norse mythologies, for instance, reflected the patriarchal realities of the Greek and Norse cultures and their manners of governance (see Mallory, 130). Following Durkheim, the French scholar Georges Dumézil argued for the existence in Indo-European mythologies of certain common forms reflecting Indo-European and, in all likelihood, proto-Indo-European cultural traditions (Mallory, 130ff). The dominant structure of Indo-European societies according to Dumézil was tripartization into classes or "functions"—religious, military, and farming and herding. In India the three functions are represented by *brahmans* (brahmins), *kṣatriyas*, and *vaiśyas*, respectively; in Iran there were *athravan, rathaestar,* and *vastriyo fsuyant*; in Rome, *flamines* (flamens), *miletes,* and *quirites*; and in Gaulish-Celtic culture, *druides, equites,* and *plebes.* This arrangement was clearly reflected in the pairing relationships of Indo-European mythologies, in which sovereign gods were related to priests and kings, warrior gods to warriors, and fertility gods to herder-farmers.

J. P. Mallory outlines the Dumézil tripartite function theory as follows:

1. The first function embraces sovereignty and is marked by a priestly stratum of society which maintains both magico-religious and legal order. The gods assigned the sovereign function are often presented as a pair, each of which reflects a specific aspect: religious such as the Indic Varuṇa or Norse Odin, and legal such as Mitra or Tyr.

2. A second military function assigned to the warrior stratum and concerned with the execution of both aggressive and defensive force, for example, the war gods Indra, Mars, and Thor.

3. A third estate conceptualizing fertility or sustenance and embracing the herder-cultivators. Here the mythic personages normally take the form of divine twins, intimately associated with horses, and accompanied by a female figure, for example, the Indic Asvins (horsemen) and Sarasvati, the Greek Castor and Pollox with Helen, the Norse Frey, Freyr, and Njorth. (132)

In relation to the third function, Jaan Puhvel follows an archeological and linguistic path to what he sees as a proto-Indo-European myth involving the mating of a noblewoman and a horse to produce divine twins. In support of his theory, he points

to an Indic horse ceremony involving sacred intoxication and to
the connection between the word for this ceremony, *áśvamedha*
(269 ff), which can be traced back to a proto-Indo-European
term meaning horse-drunk, and forward to various later Indo-
European words that are clearly related to the English word mead.
Crucial to the horse-twin myth is the sacrifice of the horse or of
one of the twins, the body of which becomes the world or is dis-
tributed to three deities (Mallory, 136–7).

Sacrifice, the source here of creation itself, is, of course, a primary theme in Indo-European mythology from Vedism to Christianity. An example of the sacrificed twin as the material for creation occurs in the Vedic myth of the first man: Manu, who in
the sacred ritual of sacrifice becomes the first priest (brahman),
and his sacrificed twin, Yemo, who, as the essence of the world
itself, becomes the first sacred king. The status of each class of
being is indicated by the part of the twin's body from which it
emerges:

> The priest was his mouth, the warrior was made from his
> arms;
> His thighs were the commoner, and the servant was born
> from his feet. (*Ṛgveda*, 10.90.11–14, in Lincoln, 7:199)

Related to the theme of sacrifice is the whole question of
death and life after death. In proto-Indo-European thought, the
death of an individual may well have been a reflection of the
greater sacrifice that was the basis of creation. Thus, we return to
the earth as a sacrifice, only later to take on new life in some
sense. Bruce Lincoln outlines four essential principles behind the
Indo-European death concept:

> (1) matter is indestructible; (2) matter is infinitely trans-
> mutable; (3) living organisms and the physical universe
> are composed of one and the same material substance;

(4) time is eternal. While change is thus constant, it is also meaningless, for nothing that is essentially real is ever created or destroyed. Worlds come and go, as do individuals of whatever species, but being—material being—is always there. (Lincoln, 7:203)

The individual role in the cosmic ritual of existence is represented mythologically in the person of the hero. Any reader of European and Indian mythology will be struck by the importance, for instance, of the theme of the cattle raid, a practice mentioned above as indicated by archeological studies of proto-Indo-European cultures. From linguistic evidence and later Indo-European myths, including examples from India, Iran, Hittite Anatolia, Greece, and the European north, Bruce Lincoln reconstructs an essential proto-Indo-European myth of the cattle raid. The myth is dominated by a hero rather than a priest—priests being more clearly associated with the practice of sacrifice (although heroism and priesthood could be combined, as in the later cases of Jesus and Buddha). The hero Lincoln calls Trito (Third), possesses a significant herd of cattle that is stolen by a non-Indo-European three-headed monster. In time, Trito, assisted by the Indo-European warrior god, overcomes the monster and takes back his cattle. The point of the myth seems to be that foreigners steal while Indo-Europeans raid. The former activity is demeaning, the latter is noble. To put it in contemporary Indo-European terms, bad raiders are terrorists, good raiders are freedom fighters. The importance of the cattle raid theme will become evident in later chapters that consider the mythologies of particular cultures, especially the Irish.

An important Indo-European hero theme with probable antecedents in proto-Indo-European society is that of the hero's struggle with and defeat of the serpent. Whereas the serpent for Neolithic peoples seems to have been associated with fertility and deep earth knowledge, for the Indo-Europeans it is clearly a representation of the kind of blind, terrestrial, animal power that must be defeated by the enlightened sky god and/or his warrior-hero representative.

The ancient Indian *Bhāgavata Purāṇa* contains this myth of Krsna, the incarnation of the great god Visnu, and his struggle with the serpent-monster Kaliya, a struggle that will be repeated in many forms by the saints and dragons, the heroes and serpents of later Indo-European cultures. Krsna's underwater struggle especially resembles the much later one of the Anglo-Saxon Beowulf and the mother of the monster Grendel. As the protector of cattle and the victor over evil represented by the serpent, he also points to Jesus as the shepherd of human sheep and the harrower of Hell.

Krsna and Kāliya

The boy Krsna went one day with his friends, the Gopīs (cowherds), to the Yamunā River. The Gopīs and their cows were so parched by the heat of the day that they drank from the river that had been poisoned by the serpent-monster Kāliya who lived beneath the water there. The Gopīs and the cows fainted from the pollution but were revived by a mere glance from Lord Krsna. Deciding to take direct action against Kāliya, Krsna climbed a kadama tree and, after clapping his hands and tightening his loin cloth, dove into the river. The turmoil caused by the dive, and the fact that Krsna frolicked in Kāliya's particular dwelling pool like an elephant, destroyed the monster's home and enraged him. Kāliya attacked Krsna with all his might, wrapping his horrible coils around him. Krsna appeared to have been utterly defeated by the serpent. The Gopīs and their herds were miserable in their grief, thinking their lord, to whom they had dedicated their lives and their possessions, was dead.

Meanwhile, back in the village, there were many portents of evil and Krsna's foster father, Nanda, became worried, as the boy had gone off without his brother Balarāma, who could always be depended upon as

a protector. The villagers and Kṛṣṇa's other friends did not realize that
Kṛṣṇa was, in fact, an incarnation of the great god Viṣṇu. Rushing to
the river, they saw their beloved Kṛṣṇa trapped in the serpent's coils,
and the women went to the boy's mother and wailed over their loss.
Nanda and others were about to dive into the pool to retrieve the body
of their young lord, but Balarama prevented them, knowing who his
brother was and that the monster serpent could not harm him.

Kṛṣṇa now saw how unhappy his friends were, rose up out of the ser-
pent's grip and proceeded to dance on the beast's hundred heads, de-
stroying each one, as poison spewed from its body. So it was that Lord
Kṛṣṇa overcame the evil that was Kāliya (see O'Flaherty, 223–6).

Many other European mythic themes would seem to have originated in some proto-Indo-European culture. Bruce Lincoln and
Cristiano Grottanelli, for instance, have isolated a theme that
concerns the commoner in victorious opposition to the priestly
or warrior class. In one myth, a humble woman, the mother of
sacred twins and the symbol of earthly fertility, wins a definitive
battle with warrior and kingly power (Lincoln, 7:200). Elements
of this theme are found throughout European mythology culminating, for example, in the struggles between Jesus and kingly and
priestly power.

Apocalyptic battles are still another Indo-European theme.
J. P. Mallory points to "striking parallels" between the great wars
between the Pāṇḍavas and the Kauravas in the Indian epic the
Mahābhārata, between the Aesir and the Vanir in Norse mythology,
and between the Sabines and the sacred Roman twins, Romulus
and Remus (139). This dualism in Indo-European mythological
structure is ubiquitous, one indicated not only by twins such as
those mentioned above but by twinned gods—Varuṇa-Mitra in
Vedic India, Odin-Tyr in northern Europe. Claude Lévi-Strauss
attributes the binary aspect to the human need to mediate between opposites (see Mallory, 141).

There is much argument among scholars as to the nature of

and/or existence of a proto-Indo-European culture. What can be said for certain is that there were several stages of conquest and migration from the north into the established cultures of the Bronze Age in Europe, Anatolia, Iran, and India; that the conquerors and migrants brought a body of myths with them; that these myths reflected the patriarchal, hierarchical, and warlike social and political structures of the conquerors; and that the new gods, goddesses, and heroes undermined but did not completely eliminate the ones they found in the lands they invaded. Thus, in the mythologies that emerged from the various cultures that evolved over the centuries in areas originally conquered by the northern invaders we find a dominance of the proto-Indo-European themes outlined above, with a lingering strain of the primary themes of the old mythology of the sedentary agriculturalists. Consider this story from the Babylonian *Enuma Elish*, a creation myth from Mesopotamia, in which patriarchal military force—in this case Semitic rather than Indo-European—overpowers a chthonic and feminine earth force turned into a monster.

Marduk and Tiamat

"The Old Hag has made the Worm! She has loosed the Dragon, the Female Monsters, the Mad Dog, Scorpion Man, the howling storm! She loathes us all, our mother Tiamat. Her horrid new brood, with venom in their veins, plot furiously against us, snarling!"

Thus did the gods, the children of Tiamat the Sea, bewail the traitorous malevolence of their mother as they met not for the first time in the Hall of the Synod to ponder their destiny in the early inchoate world.

"With their pitiless weapons, these monsters she has hatched, these eleven unflinching monsters, are led by Kingu whom she has taken as husband and made supreme. On Kingu's chest she has fastened the bronze tablets of fate. The horrid monsters now surge up from the raging sea, from the blind Old Hag, and none of us has been able to confront her."

Then Marduk stood up, among the most recent of their lineage, and said, "If I must be the avenger, if I must go kill Tiamat and save all your lives, then you must give me supreme precedence over all. My decrees shall be unalterable, never to be annulled, and my creation will extend to the very ends of the earth. I shall decide the nature of the world."

The assembled gods agreed. If Marduk could avenge them, he was king of the entire universe. They gave him the scepter, helped him onto the throne, and bestowed on him matchless weapons of war. But Marduk made his own weapon—a bow, strung with an arrow, and a mace. Then he armed himself with a net and with an atrocious wind, the hurricane, and, burning with a terrifying light as if from within, he set forth with the winds towering behind him.

He approached the Deep, Tiamat, wallowing in blind fury, and she spat out her bitter disdain. "Upstart," she roared. "Do you imagine yourself to be so great?"

"You have mothered war itself," Marduk accused. "You've given that pathetic bungler, Kingu, the rank of a leader, and you have abused the gods. Stand up, then, and we will fight it out, you and I."

Tiamat shrieked, seized with hate, trembling with malevolence, but Marduk hurled his net and caught her in it. He unleashed the atrocious wind in her face and she lunged, mouth agape, to swallow him. But Marduk drove the wind into her mouth so that she could not close it, and the wind filled her belly to bursting. Next, Marduk shot an arrow that pierced her stomach and split her heart. She sank, dying, moaning in agony, and Marduk stood astride her.

The monsters of Tiamat cowered and fled but soon found themselves enmeshed in the wise Marduk's net, then flung—along with Kingu—into the infernal realms of the underworld. Turning back to the corpse of Tiamat, Marduk smashed her skull with his mace and severed her arteries so that her blood flowed to the ends of the earth. While the gods applauded, he cut the body in two, constructing from one half the arc of the sky, from the other the solid earth.

He stretched out the immensity of the heavenly firmament and made palaces for the gods, each in its constellation. He marked out the limits of the year, giving the sun instructions to complete its annual cycle, and provided the moon with a bright jewel with which to do his nocturnal work. He scooped up the spittle from Tiamat's dead mouth and tossed it high, to become the clouds, the spindrift of the oceans, the wet wind, and the life-giving rain.

And with the world formed, Marduk set out to create in it something that would make the gods rejoice. He brought forth the rivers and plants and wild animals and then created mankind. And the hearts of the gods leapt to see this creation. (Leeming/Page, *God*, 124–7)

In Europe, which is the particular concern of this study, there is a clear development in mythology and religion, from the deeds of complex pantheons marked by patriarchy, power, and hierarchy to a single father god and his warlike, heroic followers. But always, as the myths and mythologies that form the body of this book will reveal, the old conquered, earth-based goddess and her associates continue struggling to be heard. They can be suppressed but never, if life is to go on, eliminated. During the Bronze and Iron Ages, Europe was the setting for the emergence of several rich, mythological traditions that reflected particular cultural versions of Indo-European religious ideas, social arrangements, and in many cases the religious systems of the conquered people of Old Europe. It is to these particular traditions that we turn now.

PART 2

The European Cultures
and Their Pantheons

3

Greek Mythology

W ITH THE POSSIBLE exception of the Vedic-Hindu religion of India, the religion or religions associated
with the ancient Greeks produced the world's most
complex and sophisticated mythology. Usually the Greek myths
are read as individual stories. Only when we read them all in a
book such as Robert Graves's *Greek Myths* do we become aware
that Greek mythology is, in fact, a single, gradually composed
saga of the folk imagination and many talented authors, in which
characters and events from the beginning of conceived time are
interrelated in a complex web that touches on every imaginable
aspect of the human experience.

The Aegeans: Cycladic, Minoan

The early mythology of the ancient Greeks, that of the so-called
archaic and classical periods of the middle and late Iron Age, was
preceded by several Bronze Age or Helladic stages attached to particular geographic areas in the land we now call Greece. Linguistic
evidence and the Greek historical tradition suggests that at the end
of the third millennium B.C.E. Indo-Europeans intruded upon peo-

ples whose languages and culture were primarily if not exclusively non-Indo-European. These indigenous peoples are often referred to as Aegean or, by those who argue for an earlier pre-Greek but Indo-European intrusion, as Pelasgian after Pelasgus, the first man of the ancient creation story retold below. Somewhat later arrivals in Greece are referred to as Danaans, a name taken from the story of Danaus and his many daughters, who, according to one hypothesis, brought agriculture and the fertility mysteries of the goddess Demeter to Greece from the Middle East (Graves, 1:200ff). Fragments from Apollonius of Rhodes and others suggest that the mythology of these Aegean peoples was, in fact, dominated by a mother goddess who was the source of all existence. Evidence in caves near Delphi, for instance, indicates goddess worship there dating at least from 4000 B.C.E. By 1400 B.C.E. Gaia, the personification of earth (Eurynome or Gaia), seems to have been the central focus of worship at Delphi. It was not until the eighth century B.C.E. that the Gaia cult was replaced by that of the male god Apollo. Certainly the goddess was central to the Pelasgian creation.

The Pelasgian Creation

In the beginning the great goddess Eurynome emerged from the void and had nothing to dance upon but the sea, which she separated from the sky. When she danced facing the south her movement created the North Wind, which she rubbed in her hands to form the great serpent Ophion. As she continued to dance, with increasing vitality, the serpent became aroused and mated with his creatrix. So it is that mares are said to become pregnant without the aid of a stallion, simply by turning their hindquarters to the North Wind.

Now Eurynome became a dove and eventually she laid the primal world egg of creation. She commanded Ophion to coil seven times around the egg to cause it to hatch. This he did, and all creation sprang forth—the sun, the moon, the mountains, the rivers—all of Eurynome's children.

> *The first couple moved to Mount Olympus, but Ophion resented his wife's claiming to be the creator of all things and became threatening. Eurynome would have none of this, and after bruising his head with her heel and kicking out his teeth, exiled him to the depths below earth's surface.*
>
> *The goddess now created the Titans and Titanesses and the first man, Pelasgus, the source of the Pelasgians, who came from the dark earth of Arcadia, and who taught his followers how to survive in the world.* (based on a reconstruction by Robert Graves; see Graves, 1:27).

Two cultural systems of the pre-Greek period, each also dominated by a goddess, are of particular interest. These are the so-called Cycladic, named for the group of islands between Europe and Asia, and the Minoan, the culture of ancient Crete that takes its name from the legendary King Minos.

Burial sites dating from the Cycladic culture (the third millennium B.C.E.) contain a large number of nude female figurines, some with birdlike heads, many with stylized pubic triangles, all reminiscent of the fertility goddess figures of the prehistoric period in continental Europe and Asia Minor. Further archeological evidence in the form of frescoes suggests the strong influence of nearby Crete and by about 2000 B.C.E. of Mycenaean culture and religion, although the female figure, now decorated in the Mycenaean style, continues to dominate.

The culture of Crete was also apparently goddess centered. The name Minos (perhaps Moon Man) seems to have been applied to all Cretan kings beginning about 2000 B.C.E., when Minoan civilization reached its highest point. It is possible that the title derives from the ritual marriage of each priest-king with the moon-priestess, the representative of the great Cretan goddess (Graves, 1:295). Archeological evidence in the frescoes and objects found in the famous palaces of Knossos and other settlements of Crete, as well as in caves and mountain sanctuaries of the island, suggests that the goddess herself, like her probable Near Eastern and/or European Neolithic equivalents and antecedents, was a nature deity associated with the creative essence of the earth, the cycles of nature and of life itself, including death. She is usually bare-breasted, wearing a flounced dress. Her pubic area, like that of the old Neolithic goddess, is sometimes a stylized triangle. She is depicted in many contexts, leading some scholars to suppose a Cretan pantheon made up of a snake goddess, a sea goddess, a mountain goddess, a hunting goddess, and a tree goddess, all later given specific names such as Britomartis (sweet virgin), or Ariadne (the holy one) by the Greeks, who also made connections between these figures and their own goddesses such as Demeter, Artemis, Athena, and Aphrodite. Whether one or more goddesses, the deity in question or her earthly representatives are often seen dancing in fields of flowers, accompanied by animals. A common companion is a youthful male figure whom the later Greeks associated with Zeus as a boy and who also is perhaps a form of Dionysos, a son of Zeus (dios-nusos = Zeus-like). In Crete this figure was a dying god

An ancient Cretan seal shows the goddess, full-breasted, standing on the world mountain, flanked by lions, and being adored by an aroused youth, in all likelihood the new son-lover, the new king who comes to her and will one day be the death-seed of life. Drawing by Jake Page, after G. Rachel Levy.

perhaps related to ritual sacrifice leading to fertility and renewal (see Puhvel, 137). Also present in many cases is the mysterious double ax so prevalent in Minoan symbology and a tree or pillar apparently representing divinity.

An important aspect of the Cretan goddess mythology involved the bull, possibly as a god and certainly as a sacrificial animal. It was said that the Cretan Zeus in the form of a bull, and Europa, whose name, meaning wide faced, was used as a synonym for the moon, were the parents of the original Minos. In the Neolithic period of the Near East, the goddess-bull association is made evident by archeological discoveries in Anatolia and sacred texts in Egypt. In Egypt, for instance, the moon-goddess Hathor was also the cow-goddess, and the god-king or pharaoh was the sacred bull. Much later, in the Irish *Táin* a connection is established between a great bull and a queen. In Crete a ritualized coupling of the priest-king, whose emblem was a bull, and the moon-priestess is perhaps further reflected in the story of Pasiphae, the wife of Minos, and her infatuation with a great bull.

Pasiphae and the Bull

King Minos proclaimed himself King of Crete and justified his action by boasting that he was favored by the gods and would be given whatever he prayed for. After dedicating an altar to Poseidon, he asked that a bull come to him from the sea to serve as a sacrifice to the gods. But when a beautiful white bull burst forth from the depths, he so admired it that he placed it among his own herds and substituted an inferior bull for the sacrifice.

But the gods do not appreciate or ignore such duplicity. Poseidon caused Minos's wife, Pasiphae, to lust after the great white bull. She became so desperate that she confided her passion to the superb craftsman Daedalus, who lived on the island of Knossos and carved beautiful lifelike dolls for the royal family of Crete. To help the queen, Daedalus carved a hollow wooden cow and placed it in the field where the great bull was grazing. Pasiphae slipped into the false cow, thus-

ting her legs into the cow's hollow hind legs and placing herself back
first against an opening left under the cow's tail. The white bull soon
mounted the cow and gave Pasiphae the pleasure she desired. He also
impregnated her with the Minotaur, a monstrous combination of a
bull's head with a human's body (see Graves, 1:293).

One result of Pasiphae's union with the bull was the famous
Minotaur lair, the Labyrinth, also created by Daedalus. He would
later craft the wings to allow him to escape from Crete with his
unfortunate son Icarus, whose adolescent daredevil flying would
cause his death.

The defeat of the Minotaur by the Greek hero Theseus can
serve as a metaphorical rendering of the intrusion in about 1450
B.C.E. of the Greek-speaking Mycenaeans into Crete. Many versions of the story exist. In one it is said that Theseus's human father (as opposed to his divine one, Poseidon) was persuaded by
his wife, Medea (the witchlike former wife of Jason of the Ar-
gonauts), to send Theseus to kill the famous white bull of
Minos, which had been brought to Greece by the laboring Herakles. When Theseus succeeded in killing the bull, much to the
displeasure of Medea who hoped to put her own son on the
Athenian throne, King Minos of Crete demanded that on every
ninth year he be sent seven Athenian boys and seven Athenian
maidens to be fed to the Minotaur (Asterius) in his Labyrinth.
Theseus offered himself as one of the victims and sailed with the
thirteen other victims to Crete. When the party arrived, Minos
lusted after one of the maidens and was about to rape her when
Theseus, invoking the laws of Poseidon, intervened. Minos challenged him to prove his special relationship with Poseidon, threw
his signet ring into the sea, and commanded the young hero to
find it. With the help of dolphins and other underwater followers of Poseidon, Theseus was able to retrieve the ring. Minos's
daughter Ariadne was apparently so impressed by the Athenian
that she fell in love with him and helped in what would be his
battle with the Minotaur. She gave Theseus a magic ball of

thread that had been given to her by Daedalus. She instructed him to tie one end to the Labyrinth entrance door lintel and to unravel the thread as he worked his way to the center. Once there, he was to kill the Minotaur and offer him as a sacrifice to Poseidon. When Theseus emerged victorious from the Labyrinth, he was greeted by the infatuated Ariadne, who led the Athenians to their ship and sailed away with them as Theseus's wife. After a sea battle, the party found their way to the island of Naxos, where Theseus left Ariadne and sailed for Athens. Ariadne was comforted by the god Dionysos.

The Mycenaeans

The warlike Indo-Europeans, who invaded mainland Greece during the middle of the Bronze Age (ca. 2000) and whose language would evolve into a form of Greek, brought with them the horse and chariot, advanced weapons, and the tradition of tumulus burial, as well as mythological elements of the Indo-European tradition. They became the Achaeans or Mycenaeans, the people of Agamemnon and Clytemnestra of Mycenae, Menalaus and Helen of Sparta, and, by association, Odysseus and Penelope of Ithaca. These are the familiar Greek as opposed to Trojan characters of the *Iliad* and *Odyssey* by the Homeric poet or poets who would live many centuries later. By 1600 B.C.E. the Mycenaeans ruled the Greek mainland. Meanwhile, on Crete the Minoans were building their great palaces at Knossos and for several hundred years had possessed a form of writing we know as Linear A. We know that Greek-speakers—undoubtedly the Mycenaeans—overpowered the Cretans in about 1450 B.C.E. and that they created typically Mycenaean citadels there soon afterward. By 1300 B.C.E. they had applied their own language rather awkwardly to the Linear A system and created so-called Linear B, a Greek language script useful for such things as inventories and other lists but not appropriate for literary purposes. Among the Linear B tablets, deciphered in 1953 by John Chadwick and Michael Ventris, are lists of offerings to gods. These lists indicate a radical shift away from a goddess-based mythology and religion to one presided over by the god Zeus. In Linear B, then, we discover a pre-Homeric and preclassical Mycenaean-Minoan version of what we think of as Greek mythology, the product of the indigenous peoples of Greece, the Minoans, the Indo-European tradition of the Mycenaeans, and the always present influence of the Near East. Much later this mythology would, of course, be pruned and adapted to various conditions and needs by Homer, the writers of the Homeric hymns, Hesiod, Pindar, and many others, including the dramatists of fifth-century Athens. Although knowledge of the nature and deeds of these early Olympians of Linear B is sketchy, a definable and familiar pantheon does emerge.

Offerings listed on Linear B tablets for the various deities indicate the hierarchy. Zeus (*Diwe*) reigns supreme. Hera (*Era*) is present, as are Poseidon (*Posedaone*), Athena (*Atana potinija*), Apollo (*Pajawone*), Artemis (*Atemito*), Hermes (*Emaa*), Ares (*Are* or *Enuwarijo*), Hephaistos (*Apaitioji*), Dionysos (*Diwonusojo*), and perhaps a form of Demeter (*Da-mater*) whose name means Earth Mother and who, with her daughter Persephone, might be associated with the inscription *Potniai* (Ladies), the descendants of the earlier Great Mother of Crete (Lady of the Labyrinth) and the Neolithic tradition. The missing figure here is Aphrodite, who, according to Jaan Puhvel and others, was a late, post-Mycenaean, arrival in Greece from Phoenicia via Cyprus, a version of the Semitic Astarte (Puhvel, 129–30).

Mycenaean society was characterized by a peasantry pursuing herding and relatively primitive agriculture, ruled over by a warrior aristocracy for whom raiding and conquest were appropriate paths to hero status. Monumental citadel architecture, such as that at Mycenae itself with its impressive Lion Gate and beehive tombs, and the celebration of heroic deeds in story were logical expressions of such a society. In spite of much that is outdated in

Martin Nilsson's *The Mycenaean Origin of Greek Mythology* (1932), Nilsson seems correct in seeing Mycenaean civilization as a friendly breeding ground for heroic epics and myths that would form the oral tradition out of which such works as the later Homeric epics would emerge (22). In this light one could argue, as many have, that the *Iliad* and parts of the *Odyssey* are a depiction, passed down by legend, myth, and other word-of-mouth means over several centuries, of centralized Mycenaean feudal warrior society at its height before it collapsed.

The Mycenaean collapse was due to many causes, including the intrusion of a new wave of warrior-pastoralists from southwestern Macedonia called the Dorians in the twelfth century B.C.E. One of the Dorian tribes was said to have descended from the hero Herakles, and Dorian methods reflected that hero's crude power. Following the Dorian invasion there was a long dark age characterized by small isolated, colonized, often enslaved, communities eking out a living from the soil and a decline of writing and other arts.

Archaic Greece

Homer's *Odyssey*, dominated by the sad wanderings of the old soldier Odysseus, gives some voice to the postwar disillusionment that might well have followed the Mycenaean collapse, a collapse perhaps ironically mirrored in the earlier, thirteenth century B.C.E. fall of Troy that is the subject of the *Iliad* and other tales. But in some ways the epic also reflects the new age of migration and advancement that began in the mid-ninth century B.C.E., a period of several developments that marked a Greek awakening from the dark age. A revival of interest in the past took place; the migrations over the centuries of people from the lands conquered by the Dorians, especially to Athens, the city that would become the cultural center of Greece, and from there to Ionia in Asia Minor revived a seafaring and colonizing spirit.

A Greek alphabetic writing was established along with structural changes in the language that made it more precise and more flexible, more suited to great poetry. This was the period of the legendary Homer, when the great oral epics acquired something resembling their present form and Greek mythology as we know it began to come into full literary flower. Elements of both postwar disillusionment and the cultural revival are, in fact, contained in the opening lines of the *Odyssey*:

> Let me tell the tale through you, Muse,
> The story of that man of all skills,
> Forced to wander to the ends of the earth
> Haunted by the glory days of holy Troy. (I, 1–2)

Both Homeric epics, the *Iliad* and the *Odyssey*, would serve the later Greeks as vehicles for the celebration of a hero cult in which figures of a mythical past, who mingled with and were often sired by the gods, were bigger, braver, and more beautiful than ordinary humans. These characters, whom the seventh-century B.C.E. poet and myth-maker Hesiod called "the divine race of heroes," became associated with particular places and societies in Asia Minor and Greece, their tombs—often on ancient Mycenaean sites—serving as unifying sacred centers.

The much-argued Homeric question makes it evident that a single poet named Homer might never have existed. The fact that so many places claim him as a son—Chios, Athens, Ionian Asia Minor, to mention only a few—makes him somehow the property of all Greece. In all likelihood, the work of Homer—especially the epic of wandering, the *Odyssey*—was at least in part a product of the Ionian migrations, with even eastern influence indicated by the sometimes sympathetic treatment of the Trojans in the *Iliad*.

Whether two Homers, a whole guild of Homeric bards, or one Homer composed the *Iliad* and the *Odyssey*, these works, with the seventh and sixth century B.C.E. Homeric hymns by the Homeridae (Sons of Homer), and the works of Hesiod—especially his creation story in *Theogony*—are the sourcebooks for much of what we know of Greek mythology of the preclassical archaic period.

Homer himself quickly became a part of Greek mythology, a mysterious blind bard admired by all the ancient world. In the blind Demodokos of Phaiakia, who sings the story of the Trojan War in the eighth book of the *Odyssey*, the poet, whoever he was, through his hero Odysseus, himself a great spinner of tales, praises the art of minstrelsy represented by Demodokos. He either paints a self-portrait or gives life to a myth that has intrigued humanity for over two thousand years:

Now came the court crier, leading the favored bard,
The singer loved by the Muse, who gave him good and evil—
the power of song and the absence of sight.
...

When his thirst was quenched and his hunger fed
He sang through the Muse a song of heroes,
A song known by all, far and wide.
...

Carving a piece from his chine of boar,
Odysseus called out to the blind poet's guide.
...

Pray give this meat to Demodokos,
And grant him peace from unhappy me.
Much honor is owed to the bards,
Men loved by the Muse who gives them song.

The guide took the meat, and gave it to the bard,
Whose heart was full of joy. (VIII 65–7, 75–7, 75–84)

Classical Greece

Greeks of the later classical period used Homer, the Homeric hymns, and Hesiod as history sources in schools, and the body of Greek mythology continued to grow and become more elaborate, especially in the fifth-century B.C.E. hands of the great Athenian dramatists Aeschylus, Sophocles, Euripides, and Aristophanés, and the poet Pindar. When we speak of Greek mythology, we generally refer to the accumulated body of material that would have been known to Aristotle and Alexander the Great at the beginning of the so-called Hellenistic Age in the fourth century B.C.E., with some augmentation from such later literary figures as Apollonius of Rhodes and Apollodoros, whose works owe much to the stories told by the early fifth-century B.C.E. writer Pherecydes of Leros.

It should be noted, however, that until the Hellenistic period when Apollodorus, Hyginus, Diodurus Siculus, and others collected myths more as an intellectual than a religious exercise, there was no single compilation of Greek mythology that could be compared, for instance, to the Bible or to the Vedas and other collections of India. The myths were not necessarily doctrinal in any sense. They were part of a common spiritual heritage, taught to children by the women of the household and later interpreted and questioned by teachers and philosophers such as Socrates, Plato, Aristotle, and by writers and dramatists such as those mentioned above. If there was any sense of a canonical source, it would have been centered on the ancient works of Homer, the Homeridae, and Hesiod. More important is the fact that out of this canon—which itself reached back through earlier sources both to the ancient Indo-European myth patterns and to some extent to the pre-Indo-European mythologies of the eastern and western Mediterranean—emerged a rich and complex mythological tradition that reflected a uniquely Greek view of humanity and of the relation of humanity to the inexplicable forces of the universe. At the center of this tradition is the pantheon known as the 12 Olympians, the family of gods and goddesses that dominates the classical Greek religion, a religion that to a great extent transcended differences between local practices and traditions.

The eventual arrangement of the Olympian gods into a relatively neat family is certainly a reflection of Mycenaean family and court arrangements. Zeus, who is associated with light, sky, and the thunderbolt, sits above all as the paterfamilias. As in the case of the great Mycenaean House of Atreus, for instance, his background and rise to power are marked by violent, sometimes cannibalistic, taboo-breaking progenitors, and to cataclysmic war (see the Greek creation myth in Part Three). He is a dispenser of often arbitrary justice, sometimes a doting father to his daughters, and nearly always a philanderer. His actions are based firmly in the patriarchal rights of the Indo-European, hierarchical social system. His sister and wife, Hera, the goddess of matrimony, is the forerunner of the nagging wife of later comedy, who watches her philandering husband's every move and takes extreme measures to assert her wifely position. A good example of Hera's coping with her husband's philandering is the myth of the unfortunate Io.

Zeus fell in love with Io, who was a priestess of Hera. When accused of infidelity by his wife, Zeus denied any inappropriate behavior and turned Io into a white cow which Hera then had tied to an olive tree at Nemea under the watchful hundred eyes of Argos. Zeus, however, could not give up Io, so he sent Hermes to put Argos to sleep with his flute music. Hermes then killed Argos and released Io, still of course, in her cow form. When Hera discovered what had happened, she had a gadfly chase poor Io from one end of the world to another. Thus various places in the ancient world took her name—for instance, Ionia, the Ionian Sea, the Bosphorus (Cow's Ford). When she got to Egypt, Zeus turned Io back into a human. The offspring of their relationship was Epaphus, who ruled Egypt and who some say was the divine bull Apis.

As is so often the case in patriarchal systems, it is the seduced woman who suffers the consequences of adultery rather than the seducer.

Zeus would later take up with a young woman, Europa, descended from Io and Epaphus, who would give her name to the continent of Europe. (From the Greek *Europe*-"Land of the Setting Sun," the West). Zeus spied Europa, playing by the seashore and immediately desired her. He turned himself into a white bull and appropriately, given his disguise, carried the maiden off to Crete, where he satisfied his desire. Among Europa's children by Zeus was Minos.

Another aspect of what the Greeks expected of women and womanhood is reflected in another sister of Zeus, the sometimes-Olympian Hestia, goddess of the hearth, who represents the patriarchal Greek ideal of the woman who says little and tends to the home. In keeping with her anonymity, there are few myths involving Hestia.

The most important of Zeus and Hera's brothers is Poseidon, the god of the sea who is also closely associated with horses and therefore perhaps with the traditional Indo-European horse mythology discussed earlier. Poseidon and Zeus and their non-Olympian brother Hades (who lives in the underworld from which he takes his name) represent the three essential powers of sky, sea, and underworld. In a bow to the ancient pre-Indo-European tradition of earth as mother, the fourth element of the arrangement of the world, earth itself, is represented by Demeter, the sister of Zeus whose name, as noted earlier, suggests motherhood. But in keeping with the patriarchal essence of the Indo-European cosmos, earth and the mother are diminished in importance, and earth and earthlings have become the playthings of the sky gods. This fact is evident, for instance, in the myth of the rape of Persephone, a story most elaborately told in the first Homeric hymn to Demeter.

I sing now of the great Demeter,
Of the beautiful hair,
And of her daughter Persephone,
Of the lovely feet,
Whom Zeus let Hades tear away
From her mother's harvests
And friends and flowers—
Especially the Narcissus,
Grown by Gaia to entice the girl
As a favor to Hades, the gloomy one.
This was the flower that
Left all amazed,
Whose hundred buds made
The sky itself smile.
When the maiden reached out
To pluck such beauty,
The earth opened up
And out burst Hades
. . .
The son of Kronos,
Who took her by force
On his chariot of gold,
To the place where so many
Long not to go.
Persephone screamed,
She called to her father,
All powerful and high,
. . .
But Zeus had allowed this.
He sat in a temple
Hearing nothing at all,
Receiving the sacrifices of
Supplicating men.

Only Hecate in her cave and the sun heard her cries. Zeus had known of his brother's plans and even approved of them. So it was that Persephone was taken by Hades down to his home to reign there as his queen.

But Demeter was, understandably, not willing to accept the rape of her daughter or the collusion of her brothers in the act. In anger and despair, she allowed the earth to fall into ruin and everyone and everything on it would have perished had Zeus not relented and convinced Hades to allow Persephone to return to her mother. The return could be for only half of each year, however, as Persephone had eaten of the food of the underworld. She had lost her innocence and contained death within herself. When she left her mother each year to return to her husband and her dark palace under the earth, Demeter became sad, and the warm, fertile seasons gave way to fall and winter.

The younger generation of the heavenly family includes several sons and daughters of Zeus by various immortals. Hermes is a trickster god who, in the Indo-European tradition, is involved in cattle raiding (as a child he stole Apollo's cows) and who leads the dead to Hades. He has a phallic aspect in the stone pillars or herms set along roads and in front of houses, perhaps to mark the way to bring luck or protection, or, as these pillars often sport erect phalluses, to ensure fertility. He is also a messenger for his father. His mother is Maia, the daughter of the Titan Atlas, best known for his holding up the world. Maia's name recalls that of the Indian Māyā, who represents illusion and magic, characteristics appropriate to the mother of a trickster.

Two sons of Zeus with Hera are less interesting than their more adventurously conceived siblings. Ares was the god of war. Hephaistos was the god of the crafts, a version of a typical Indo-European smith god such as we find playing more important roles, for instance, in both Celtic and Germanic mythology. Ares and Hephaistos are sometimes treated rather comically. Hephaistos is lame as a result of his having been flung out of heaven for having attempted to protect his mother, Hera, from Zeus's physical abuse. He is married to his highly erotic and beautiful sister Aphrodite with whom his better-looking brother Ares has an affair. Aphrodite was said to be the daughter of Zeus and the nymph Dione, but we believe now, as noted above, that she came to Greece from the east, probably as a version of the fertility goddess Astarte. Homer has the blind Demodokos tell a wonderfully comic story of Aphrodite and Ares' affair. He relates how the powerful Ares and the beautiful Aphrodite made love in the bed of Aphrodite's lame husband, and how the wronged husband prepared a trap for the lovers when he discovered their treachery. He created a netting of chains around his bed and waited hidden until the lovers were at the very height of the act of love. Then he pulled a rope that released the trap and the bed with the entwined lovers was raised to the ceiling, preventing either separation or escape. Hephaistos then called the gods together to mock the naked pair caught in their indecency.

Other Olympians of eastern origin were Apollo and his sometimes twin sister Artemis, born of the union of Zeus and Leto, a daughter of the Titans Coeus (intelligence) and Phoebe (moon). The lovers couple in the form of quails. Hera finds out about this act of infidelity and once again it is the woman who must suffer the consequences. Hera has her chased around the world, as poor Io was, but this time by the great Python, who would continue to be important in the Apollo myth. Artemis and Apollo were usually believed to have been born in Delos, but some say they were born in Ephesus or Lycia. It is this Asia Minor connection that makes appropriate Artemis' and Apollo's support of the Trojans in the *Iliad*. As anyone who has seen depictions of the many-breasted Artemis of Ephesus will realize, the Artemis whom the Greeks would see as a virginal huntress was at one time clearly a goddess of fertility.

Apollo was a complex god of many aspects, among them light,

the sun, the arts, and, as his association with the great prophetic center of Delphi would indicate, prophecy. His motto, made so poignantly relevant in the tragic story of Oedipus, is "Know thyself." Like the Vedic Indra and Rudra (later Śiva) Indo-European archer, he is a version of the god-hero who defeats the monster—in this case, the Python. Almost always the monster-dragon-serpent is associated with the chthonic powers of the ancient great mother, whose powers are then taken over by the Indo-European patriarchy. In the case of the Greeks, this takeover is indicated not only by the replacement of the goddess cult at Delphi with that of Apollo, but by the myth of the trial of Orestes at Athens for the revenge killing of his mother, Clytemnestra. At that trial, as depicted by Aeschylus in *The Eumenides*, Apollo absolves Orestes on the grounds that the mother is not the real parent, only the vessel of the seed placed there by the father.

One of the most prestigious of Zeus's children is the goddess Athena, patroness of Athens, goddess of wisdom, who, according to the first Homeric Hymn was born, appropriately, of Zeus's painfully aching head, fully and splendidly armed.

In the trial of Orestes described in *The Eumenides*, Athena represents, in her highly masculinized form, the transformation of religious power from the mysteries of the female chthonic earth to the reason of the male-dominated sky.

Finally, there is the outsider son of Zeus, the thirteenth Olympian, Dionysos. Dionysos is in some ways the most mysterious of the gods, and in his own way one of the most powerful. If we associate Apollo with the Apollonian approach to life, an approach centered on self-knowledge and moderation, we associate Dionysos with the Dionysian, the ecstatic. Both aspects are, of course, necessary to the full life (and for great art), and it is for this reason that Dionysos was said to inhabit Apollo's Delphi in the winter months.

Like Athena, Dionysos, according to Apollodorus, Apollonius

of Rhodes, and others, was born directly of Zeus. Zeus, disguised as a mortal, had a love affair with Semele (Moon), daughter of the King of Thebes. Soon Semele was pregnant with the god's son. It was the jealous Hera who, disguised as an old woman, advised the young woman to entice her lover to allow her anything she wished. When he agreed, as in the throes of passion he of course would, she was to request that he reveal himself to her in his true form. The trick worked and Zeus, who could never go back on his word, was forced to reveal himself to Semele. As no mortal can bear the power and brightness of the god of thunder and lightning, Semele was destroyed by her vision. Fortunately, Hermes saved the unborn baby and sewed it into Zeus's thigh, from which, three months later, the "twice born" god was born (see Graves, 1:56).

Another association with Zeus is suggested by the name Dionysos itself, which etymologically develops, as noted earlier, from sounds relating him directly to Zeus—Zeus-like or even Zeus's nurseling (see Puhvel, 137). It is clear that Dionysos, like several of the Greek gods, has a particularly Minoan background. Like the boy Zeus of Crete, for example, Dionysos is a dying god, and he was always considered a foreign god. Ancient writers believed that he came from Thrace, the home in the Balkans of many religiously and linguistically related tribes, including the Getae and the Dacians, who sided with Troy in the *Iliad*. In the fifth book of the *Iliad*, Homer tells how the Thracian King Lykurgos resisted Dionysos and was made insane by him, and eventually committed suicide or was killed by him. When one places this story next to that of the Thracian version of Artemis, called Cotys, a chthonic deity who made men wear women's clothes in her orgiastic rites, we cannot help but think of Euripides' *The Bacchae* and the conflict in that play between the ecstatic foreign god and the Theban King Pentheus. Pentheus, like Lykurgos, is driven mad and, dressed in women's clothes, he meets a tragic and orgiastic end. Although sometimes assimilated as an Olympian, Dionysos seems more comfortable in the company of the earth-based or activities such as those "mysteries" surrounding Demeter and Kore (Persephone) at Eleusis.

The Eleusinian mysteries represent one of several approaches to religion that were offshoots of or alternatives to the official Olympian religion known through Greek mythology. The Dionysian religion was another approach and the Orphic marked still another. The mysteries and the Dionysian religion coexisted easily enough with the civic religion. The great dramatic festivals of Athens, for example, were dedicated to Dionysos, and it was common for people of high civic stature to be associated with the Eleusinian mysteries.

Orphism, which came into its own in the Hellenistic period but which we know now existed as early as the sixth century B.C.E., was a movement that assimilated elements of the Olympian religion with those of Eleusis and Dionysos. Orphism was more a philosophy than a religion, stressing a movement in the world from cosmic order, represented mythologically by an original primordial egg, to a gradually developing disorder. The possibility of reintegration is represented by an Orphic version of Dionysos, a god who is dismembered and eaten by Titans as a baby only to be returned to life under the care of Persephone and/or Demeter. There is a strong and clear connection, as the historian Herodotus recognized, between the Dionysos-Persephone/Demeter relationship and the Egyptian resurrection god Osiris and his sister-wife Isis. This connection pointed to a Hellenistic tendency to fuse Greek gods with those of the many religious traditions in the empires of Alexander and Rome. The possibility of regeneration and rebirth that the savior Dionysos-Osiris represents is, of course, an important path to the story of Jesus as a resurrected dying man-god, a story that would eventually give new life to the ancient Indo-European theme of the necessary sacrifice and so turn the older religion of Greece into mythology.

By the time Paul and his followers made their way to the Greek colonies in Asia Minor, they found a population more than ready for the new religion. In a passage from the New Testament Acts of the Apostles (14:8–18), we are told that when at Lystra Paul cured a man who had been "lame from birth," the people cried out that "The gods have come down to us in human form!" They called one of Paul's companions Zeus, and Paul himself "they called Hermes, because he was the spokesman" (Hermes traditionally being the messenger of the gods). The priest of Zeus brought animals to be sacrificed, and even when Paul denied that he and his assistants were gods and attempted to preach their new religion of resurrection, "they barely managed to prevent the crowd from offering sacrifice to them."

4

Roman Mythology

As GREEK MYTHOLOGY cannot be separated from its background of indigenous pre-Greek cultures, Roman mythology is intricately influenced by ancient Italic cultures, especially those of other Latin tribes, the non-Indo-European Etruscans, and the Greek colonizers of Sicily and southern Italy.

The Latins

By the beginning of the first millennium B.C.E. several tribes who spoke a form of Latin lived along the Tiber in an area known as Latium Vetus (Old Latium), bordered by the Etruscan and Sabine territories. The Latins were united in the worship of the god Jupiter Latiaris, whose sanctuary was on Mons Albanus, and of the goddess Diana Aricina, whose sacred grove was in Aricia. Elaborate ritual sacrifice was made to Jupiter Latiarus. Diana, whose name is formed from the same root as Jupiter, seems to have been just as important, representing night to Jupiter's day and also demanding significant sacrifice. Later Diana, like the great goddess of Crete and the Artemis of Anatolia, would be reduced in stature. Another element of a mythological basis for this early Latin federation is suggested by a seventh-century B.C.E. burial place at Lavinium, a grave that has traditionally been considered to be that of the hero Aeneas, the central figure in one of the myths of the founding of Rome. Lavinium was also the center of the cult of Venus, the mother of Aeneas and, therefore, of Rome. This Aeneas myth is best known to us through its treatment by the poet Vergil in his epic *Aeneid*, written during the period of the emperor Augustus.

According to the tradition developed by Vergil, following Homer, Aeneas was a Trojan hero. The son of Venus by Anchises, Aeneas led various followers out of the ruins of Troy on a long journey that would culminate in the founding of the new Troy, or Rome. Along the way, Aeneas's father died and Aeneas visited him in the underworld, learning there his ultimate destiny. On his way to the new Troy, Aeneas would perhaps have given in to the love he felt for Queen Dido in Carthage and stayed there but for the prodding of his mother. His wanderings in the first half of the *Aeneid* look back to the wanderings of Odysseus in Homer's *Odyssey*. The second half of the epic, in which Aeneas fights enemies in Italy, has its formative model in Homer's *Iliad* and is a version of the great Indo-European Armageddon that we find, for instance, not only in the Trojan War, but also in the Indian *Mahabharata* and, as we shall see, in the Irish *Book of Invasions* and the Norse *Eddas*.

In his *De Republica*, Cicero restated the tradition that it was the twins Romulus and Remus—known by the Greeks as Rhomos (Rome) and Rhomulos (Roman)—sons of the god Mars and the Vestal Virgin Rhea Silvia, who founded Rome (see below). Rome, the *Urbs* (the City), was, in fact, not officially founded until 753 B.C.E. in a ceremony on the hill that the world knows as the Palatine.

Archaic Roman Mythology

Our sources for Roman mythology date primarily from the first century B.C.E. and the early first century C.E. and are found for the most part in the works of Cicero, Vergil, the historian Livy, the philosopher-historian Plutarch, and the poet Ovid. The supreme Roman god of Urbs was Iuppiter (Jupiter), whose name shares the Indo-European root Iou (whence *dyeu*) with the Greek Zeus (*dyeus*) and the Sanskrit *dyaus* (the sky). Although the early Roman gods were personal, they were generally not anthropomorphic. Many were embodiments of abstract concepts. Fides was the goddess of good faith, Ceres was the goddess of agricultural growth, Consus was the god of grain, especially in its stored form, Ops was the goddess of opulence, Janus the two-headed god of gateways or life passages, Vesta the goddess of the sacred fire. Some of the archaic deities were particularly associated with ritual celebrations. The goddesses Angerona and Mater Matuta (Aurora) were apparently known primarily through solstice celebrations.

At the center of archaic Roman mythology was a version of the Indo-European triad—in this case Jupiter-Mars-Quirinus (sovereignty-power-community). Jupiter in this context is proper sovereignty, such as that belonging to the Vedic Varuna, while Mars is pure power such as that represented in the Vedic Indra. Quirinus is a representation of peaceful Roman community marked by prosperity.

The archaic Roman triad is itself related to the Romulus and Remus myth, a crucially important Roman version of the Indo-European sacred-twins theme told by Ovid, Livy, and others.

The twins Romulus and Remus were born of the union of the god Mars and the mortal Rhea Silva. Rhea Silva, whose name suggests nature and the earth itself, had been forced into the role of Vestal Virgin by her uncle Amulius, the king, who hoped thus to keep her from producing a rival heir to the throne that he had usurped from her father, Numitor. When the twins were born, the evil king had them placed in an ark of sorts and left to float away in the Tiber. When the ark happened to run aground, a female wolf discovered the children and suckled them. Later the boys were adopted, as young heroes often are in such myths, by a shepherd. Romulus and Remus grew and became known for their strength, but one day Remus was overcome in a quarrel with his grandfather Numitor's followers and taken to Numitor to be punished. Hearing of this, Romulus went to his brother's rescue and the twins were revealed as Numitor's grandsons. The reunited family now defeated the usurper Amulius and restored Numitor to his throne. Romulus and Remus went to the place along the Tiber where they had been rescued by the wolf and there they founded Rome. A quarrel between the brothers over which one should give his name to the new city resulted in the death of Remus, and so Rome took its name from Romulus.

In the early days Rome experienced a shortage of women, a problem solved by Romulus in a deceitful manner. He invited the Sabines to a feast and then he and his followers seized and raped the Sabine women. After a long period of war between the Sabines and the Romans, a truce and alliance between the two peoples was arranged by the Sabine women themselves, who were now, after all, Roman wives and mothers. Years later, Romulus disappeared in a flash of lightning and was taken to the heavens to become a god, thus establishing a precedent for the deification of Roman rulers.

In this ancient story of Rome's founding, Remus, who is killed, serves as the sacrifice out of which, it might be said, Rome is born, much as the Vedic world is born of the dead body of Manu's twin, Yama. As Jaan Puhvel suggests, "Remus had to die as part of the act of creation, which led to the birth of the three Roman 'tribes' (Ramnes [Romans], Luceres [Etruscans], Tities [Sabines]) and the accession of Romulus to his role as first king, the saga equivalent of the anthropogonic first man" (288). The Romulus-led rape of the Sabine women represents the assimilation of a rustic culture with that of Rome and Etruria to make up an archaic Roman tripartite society. Romulus, the sacred king whom Rome eventually deified, is essential to the archaic Roman triad, as Mars was his father and Jupiter his patron, and when he finally left this world in the thunderstorm, he was identified with Quirinus. He and his twin were referred to as the *geminos quirinos* (twin quirini), recalling the Greek *Dioscuri* (sons of god) Castor and Polydeuces (Pollux).

The Etruscans

Eventually, in the seventh century B.C.E., Rome became the dominant force among the Latin cities, only to be overcome by the neighboring Etruscans, who ruled Rome through their kings until their expulsion and the formation of the Republic in 509 B.C.E. These non-Indo-European speakers possessed the most advanced civilization in Italy from the eighth to the fourth century B.C.E. Under the Etruscan kings, Rome was influenced by Etruscan religion, especially by that prophetic aspect having to do with such practices as haruspicy (the study of entrails of animals sacrificed for prophecy), divination from lightning flashes, and various related rituals, all growing out of the mythic tradition of the prophet Tages and his sacred books. It was said that Tages appeared out of a plowed furrow as a gray-haired child with the wisdom of an ancient sage to teach the people at Tarquinia. Another source for the Etruscan divination that influenced Rome was the sibyl-like nymph, the prophet Begoia. The Romans would adopt the oracular Sibylline Books, that they would consult for guidance in difficult times. One story has it that the great Sibyl of Cumae sold three of her prophetic books to King Tarquin, who deposited them on the Capitoline Hill where they were available for consultation.

Eventually, under the influence of eastern contacts, the Etruscans would accept Astarte, the ancient Phoenician great goddess whom they saw as a version of their own Uni, and of the Greek Hera and Roman Juno. Another important Etruscan goddess was Mernva (Minerva in Rome). It is significant, given their

non-Indo-European background, that the Etruscans, who regarded women and goddesses more highly than did their Indo-
European neighbors, replaced the archaic Roman and thor-
oughly Indo-European triad of Jupiter-Mars-Quirinus with that
of Jupiter, Juno, and Minerva. The new triad was represented on
a Capitoline Hill temple, and when the Roman Republic replaced the Etruscan kings, the female-dominated triad remained
in place.

The Etruscans, like the Romans, who often went so far as to
invite the gods of their enemies to become *their* gods, borrowed
easily from the mythologies of others—from their neighbors the
Latins and, because of their maritime connections, especially
from the Greeks. Foreign deities were, in effect, considered ho-
mologues for those found in Etruria. The Etruscan name for the
sovereign god (the Roman Jupiter, the Greek Zeus) was Tinia, a
god known for his powerful lightning flashes. Hera was the
Etruscan Uni, Aphrodite-Venus was a goddess of love, Turan.
Apollo and Artemis were adopted as Aplu and Artumes, Poseidon was Nethuns, Hermes was Turms, Ares (the Latin Mars)
was Maris, Athena-Minerva was Mernva, the Latin Janus was the
Etruscan Ani.

Republican Rome

Soon after the expulsion from Rome of the last Etruscan king,
Tarquin the Proud, the Romans defeated the Latin tribes at Lake
Regillus and formed a Latin League with them. A major setback
to the development of Rome was the sacking of the city by the
Gauls in the period between 387 and 390 B.C.E. The Latin alliance
was dissolved after a Latin revolt in 343–341 B.C.E., and by 338
B.C.E. the Latins had simply been absorbed by Rome.

By this time the Roman pantheon was fairly well established—
an amalgam of Latin, Etruscan, and absorbed Greek ideas. The
Romans imported certain Greek or Greco-Etruscan deities such

as Apollo, who was introduced by way of a Sibylline prophecy as a healing god early in the fifth century B.C.E., and Castor, who was adopted to support the Romans in a battle. Rome made nearly all of the major figures of its pantheon syncretic with those of the Greek, even to some extent accepting marriages in a divine family that in earlier times had not been thought of as a family. Temples dedicated to particular deities became more prominent, statuary became important, and the gods, understandably, became more anthropomorphic. Jupiter emerged as more Zeus-like and was now married to Juno, who took on a role as patroness of marriage. Some might see this as a promotion for Juno, but in the earlier Etruscan-Latin understanding she had been a version of Uni-Astarte, the great goddess, who with Jupiter and Minerva, ruled over Rome on the Capitoline Hill. In her role as Jupiter's wife, Juno did maintain at least something of an earlier status. In the story used by Vergil in the *Aeneid*, her feminine powers lie behind Dido's almost preventing Aeneas from leaving Carthage to found Rome.

As for the other gods, Mars retained a greater importance than he had possessed as Ares in Greece. He was not only a martial god but an agrarian one. Diana became a huntress, like her Greek homologue Artemis, and lost much of her early Latin importance in the process. As in some Greek versions of her myth, she was Apollo's sister. Vesta was understood to be a version of the unimportant Greek Hestia, but she took on a great deal more importance in Rome as the embodiment not only of the hearth but of the old Indo-European fire cult, now that of the Vestal Virgins. The Roman Venus, too, may have Indo-European roots. Her name perhaps looks back to the neuter Vedic term for desire, but under the Greek influence of Aphrodite, she becomes distinctly feminine. Still, as the mother of Aeneas and, therefore, a patroness of Rome, she takes on the kind of stature that Athenians gave to Pallas Athena rather than to Aphrodite, who in Greece was something of a spoiled daughter and a vamp. Athena in Rome, however, is Minerva, once closely associated with Juno, as indicated by her place with that goddess on the Capitoline. Poseidon lives on in Rome as Neptunus, Hermes as Mercurius, Hephaistos as Vulcanus, Dionysos as Bacchus.

A prime example of the effect of Greek mythology on Roman is that of the triad Ceres-Liber-Libera, which owes its very being to that of Demeter-Dionysos-Kore (Perspehone) and the story of Hades' (the Roman Pluto) rape of Persephone (the Roman Proserpina), because of which the archaic abstract Ceres became the anthropomorphic figure depicted in a statue in her temple dedicated in 493 B.C.E. near the Circus Maximus in Rome.

A useful picture of the Roman version of the Olympians is discovered in a popular rite, the *lectisternium*, in which offerings of food were made to statues of gods and goddesses displayed in pairs in temples on great beds, or *lectisternia*. This rite, developed through Senate-ordered consultation with the Sibylline Books during times of difficulty, was first practiced in 399 B.C.E. In this first *lectisternium*, the purely Greek Apollo and his mother, Latona, were positioned together in the most honored place in the hope that the healing god Apollo would overcome a severe pestilence that threatened the city. The historian Livy tells us that the last *lectisternium*, ordered in 217 B.C.E. to ward off Hannibal's attack on Rome during the Second Punic War, marked the adaptation of the Greek pattern of twelve-paired deities: Juno and Jupiter, Neptune and Minerva, Mars and Venus, Apollo and Diana, Vulcan and Vesta, Mercury and Ceres (Livy, 22.10.9). It must be pointed out that whatever the Greek meaning of these common pairs—for example, the marriage of Hera and Zeus, the erotic affair of Ares and Aphrodite, the sibling connection of Apollo and Artemis—the Romans almost certainly attached their own meaning. As Robert Schilling has noted, Juno and Jupiter had long been associated as part of the Etruscan-Roman triad in the Capitoline cult; the joining of Vulcan and Vesta referred to sacred fire, protected in Rome by the Vestal Virgins; and the pairing of Venus and Mars had a particularly Roman meaning which was more important than the Greek story of their affair (12:458). Mars was, after all, the father of Romulus and Venus the mother of Aeneas. In this pairing, the Romans succeeded in joining the two myths of the origins of Rome.

The myth of Venus as the mother of Aeneas had been augmented during the First Punic War when, during the occupation of Mount Eryx beginning in 248 B.C.E., the Romans had recognized the Aphrodite there as Venus—specifically Venus Erycina, whose temple was later built near the summit of the Capitoline. Soon after that, another Anatolian or Trojan goddess, the Anatolian Cybele, the *magna mater*, the mother of the dying god Attis (later himself celebrated in Rome), was introduced and housed in a temple on the Palatine.

Imperial Rome

The extension of Roman power and language into the world beyond the Italian peninsula was marked by assimilation of other mythologies and/or the identification of foreign gods with Roman ones. This process, as we have seen, had already begun in connection with Latin, Etruscan, and Greek deities and coincided with the mixture of Latin and vernacular languages that resulted in the Romance languages (Italian, French, Portuguese, Spanish, and Romanian). Sometimes the mythic assimilation merely involved a name change, as in the case of Venus Erycina or the later Mars Lenus in Gaul or Jupiter Dolichenus from Doliche. Deities—especially eastern ones—were also directly imported as themselves. Such deities included the goddess Ma brought from Anatolia, as the great mother Cybele already had been, and equated with Bellona. There were many examples of the Romans following their ancient tradition of enlisting the gods of enemies to fight for them. The Greek hero Herakles, for example, became Herucles Victor in 145 B.C.E. to celebrate the Roman victory over Greece.

An important development of mythology during the imperial period was that of the emperor cult. Julius Caesar had been deified by the Senate after his death in 44 B.C.E. as was Augustus, who led a religious revival, built a temple to his personal family god, Mars Ultor, as the avenger of Caesar's murder. Under Augustus's rule (31 B.C.E.–14 C.E.) the cult of the living emperor emerged, in which the emperor was thought to be guided from within by his divine element, or *genius*. For his work on earth, he would be rewarded by Jupiter with the gift of immortality. This understanding of a divine being sent into the world to save it doubtless had an effect on the thinking of early Christians, who lived during the time of Augustus.

Early Christianity found a breeding ground in Roman thought and tradition not only because of the relatively easy transference from the emperor cult to that of the Son of God, but because of the popularity in first century B.C.E. and first century C.E. of mystery cults from the east, of which Christianity was one. Mithraism, imported from Persia in the first century C.E., stressed secret communal gatherings, sacrifice, and a shared ritual meal. The emperor Gaius built a temple to the Egyptian goddess Isis, whose mystery cult was associated with the sacrificed and resurrected king-god Osiris. Earlier Cybele, the Anatolian *magna mater*, had been exalted in Rome, and later her cult was joined by that of her sometimes son, the dying god Attis.

Sir James Frazer's description of the Spring Feast of Attis cannot help but remind us of the story of the Christian man-god, whose death by hanging gave birth to a sacred ritual meal. Frazer tells us that the festival of Attis and his mother, the earth goddess Cybele, was celebrated in Rome in the spring. The trunk of a pine tree was brought to the sanctuary of Cybele, wrapped in cloth and decorated with flowers as if it were a corpse. An effigy of Attis was placed on it. On the third day of the cere-

mony—the Day of Blood—the priests of Attis cut themselves
and during a frenzied Dionysian dance splattered the "corpse"
with their blood. Frazer supposes that the novices of the priestly
order castrated themselves as a sign of loyalty to the god on the
same day that the symbolic representation of the god was placed
in a sepulcher. All the worshippers then mourned the death of
Attis until, during the night, there appeared a light and the tomb
was opened to reveal that the god had risen from the dead. The
next day—probably on the vernal equinox, the resurrection of
Attis was celebrated in a carnival-like Festival of Joy. Associated
with the mysteries of Attis was a fast, a sacramental meal, and a
belief that through Attis's resurrection the worshipper would
overcome death (see *The New Golden Bough*, 370–4).

The replacement of Greco-Roman pagan mythology with that
of Christianity was a gradual process, beginning with the missionary work of the apostle Paul to Greece and Rome and, traditionally, with the arrival of Peter in Rome during the first century C.E. The early Christian community was adamant in its
refusal to worship the emperor and the other Roman gods. Perse-
cution resulted, including, according to Christian tradition, the
hanging of Peter and Paul, but so did the community's missionary work. When, at the Battle of Milvian Bridge in October of
312 C.E, Emperor Constantine attributed his victory not to Apollo
or Hercules or Mars but to the god of the Christians, the future
dominance of Christianity in Europe was assured. Constantine
would move his capital to Byzantium, the "new Rome," renaming
it Constantinople. In 341 pagan sacrifices were prohibited and the
closing of pagan temples followed soon after that.

5

Celtic Mythology

THE ORIGIN OF the Celts, today the smallest group of Indo-European speakers, is unclear. Some archeologists have perhaps somewhat dubiously suggested the existence of a proto-Celtic Indo-European people in the so-called Beaker and Battle-Ax cultures of the third millennium B.C.E. Still others see Celtic beginnings in the urnfield and tumulus cultures of the second millennium. Claims with more basis are those made for the central European Hallstatt culture of the ninth century B.C.E., marked by the extensive use of iron, and especially the fifth century B.C.E. La Tène culture, an Indo-European aristocratic-warrior culture that existed in the European lands we generally think of as Celtic.

It is possible that Celtic peoples began their great migration from the headwaters of the Rhone, Danube, and Rhine Rivers as early as the beginning of the first millennium B.C.E. We know that in the fifth century B.C.E. the Greek writers Herodotus and Hecataeus of Miletus (in Western Anatolia) reported that by 500 B.C.E. the Celts lived in most areas of central and western Europe. Gaul, parts of Spain, Italy, the Balkans, and even Sicily, Greece, and Asia Minor, all had experienced a Celtic presence by then or would soon after. Early in the fourth century B.C.E. Celtic tribes (*Celtae* or *Galli*) overran the city of Rome and in 279 B.C.E. Celts (*Keltoi*) attacked Delphi; and soon after that, Celts (*Galatae*) penetrated Asia Minor where they founded Galatia in the area around ancient Gordion, the city of King Midas, where Alexander the Great was said to have destroyed the famous Gordion Knot.

The Celtic migrations to Britain took place from the fifth century B.C.E. to the arrival of the Belgae in the first century B.C.E. Celts were in Ireland at least as early as the third century B.C.E.

In spite of the obvious importance of the Celts in Europe during a period we associate primarily with the classical cultures of Greece and Rome, we have little direct knowledge of early Celtic mythology. This is because, although Celts had contact with the highly literate Greeks as early as 600 B.C.E. in what is now southern France, their druidic priests disdained writing as a means of transmitting sacred text. In this belief in the primacy of oral transmission, the druids resembled their Indo-European relatives in India, the brahmans, for whom works such as the Vedas were *śruti*, that is, "heard" revelation rather than mere *smṛti*, texts contaminated by human influence.

Continental Celtic myths, then, were essentially not written down until the first century B.C.E. by the Romans, including, among others, Posidonius, Diodorus Siculus, Strabo, Lucan, Tacitus, and especially Julius Caesar in his *De Bello Gallico* (Gallic Wars), a history of the Roman conquest of Gaul (58–51 B.C.E.). As for the mythology of the British Isles, it was not until sometime after the advent of Christianity there—perhaps as late as the sixth century C.E.—that Irish monks produced the manuscripts that would preserve the traditions of their homeland. Our primary access to Celtic mythology, then, is through the eyes and minds of Romans, who tended to associate the deities of the conquered with their own pantheon, and through Christian writers, who at least to some extent sought ways to reconcile ancient Celtic traditions with those of the new religion.

Continental, Gallo-Romano Celts

A good example of the inevitable Roman distortion of the Gaulish pantheon is Caesar's listing of the Celtic gods with Roman
rather than Celtic names. He tells us that Mercury is the most
worshiped god of Gaul, that he is the god of arts, crafts, and
commerce and journeys. Next in rank, he says, are Apollo, who
cures disease; Mars, the god of War; Jupiter, who rules the heavens; and Minerva, who teaches the arts and crafts. (6: 17).

If Caesar believed Mercury to be the most worshiped of the
Celtic gods, it was because his terra cotta and stone images pre-
dominated in Gaul. Sometimes he appears with three heads, reminding us of the Indo-European triad, and sometimes he has a
consort called Maia or Rosemerta (Provider). As for Caesar's
Gaulish Mars, he seems to be represented as a god of healing as
well as of war. Caesar's Celtic Apollo is, in fact, a composite of
several deities, some of whom are a solar god Belenus, another
solar god named Grannus, whose consort was Sirona, and a god
of thermal springs called Bormo, who was associated with Da-
mona, one of the Indo-European world's many sacred bovine
goddesses. Caesar's Minerva was another thermal springs goddess, Sulis, in Gaul. But she was probably much more. Often
called Belisama (Brightest), she was in all likelihood the Celtic
great goddess, other versions of which we find in Irish mythology representing sovereignty and the land itself.

Various Roman interpreters provided differing versions of
the Gaulish pantheon. Three figures stand out in these interpre-
tations. Lucan mentions "harsh Teutates," "dread Esus," and
"Taranis," Celtic deities or deity types. All three gods demanded
brutal sacrifice. The victims of the three gods were drowned,
hanged, and burned, respectively. Teutates, like Esus, was considered by the Romans to be equivalent to either Mercury or Mars.
Taranis was either Jupiter or another name for Dispater (Dis
Pater), the ruler of the Otherworld (*dis* being the Latin word for

the Greek Hades), whom, according to Caesar, the Gauls thought of as their ancestor. There may be an etymological connection here with the proto-Indo-European *Dis* from *Dyaus* (sky)—thus *Dis Pater* (sky father). Some scholars have seen these three gods as in reality aspects of a single deity (Mac Cana, "Celtic Religion," 3:152). The three-headed Mercury mentioned above perhaps lends credence to this interpretation. Jaan Puhvel points out that Teutates is derived from the Celtic term for "people"—thus Teutates is the People's God—that Esus means "Lord," and that Taranis can be associated etymologically with "thunder" (169).

The Indo-European tripartite arrangement of king/priest-warrior-people is at least reflected here. Single-deity people have assumed an Indo-European triadic relationship for these gods— a Celtic trinity equivalent to the Roman Jupiter-Mars-Quirinus discussed earlier. Puhvel, however, doubts this interpretation, preferring to see Esus as the equivalent of Caesar's most worshiped Mercury—the high god of the Celtic pantheon. For Puhvel, Esus-Taranis-Teutates are a triad resembling not so much the Roman triad as that of the also sacrifice-demanding Germanic Odin-Thor-Freyer triad to be discussed later (169–70).

Insular Celts

The Celts who came to the British Isles in waves beginning as early as the sixth century B.C.E. were Gaels (Goidels), the ancestors of the Celtic peoples who still inhabit Ireland and Scotland, and the Cymri, Brythons (Britons), and Belgae, whose descendants can be found in Wales and Cornwall (as well as in Brittany in France). The word *British* is a derivation of the old Breton *Brytass*, a synonym for the insular Celts.

The invading Celts displaced but were certainly influenced by the religious and mythological traditions of earlier peoples, the builders of stone circles such as Stonehenge. The Celts themselves were challenged by the tentative invasion of Julius Caesar in the mid-first century B.C.E. and were conquered by Rome a century later. Roman influence on Celtic religion and mythology is evident in all parts of Britain. But by about 300 C.E. Roman Britain had begun to be attacked by Germanic peoples, and by the middle of the fifth century c.e. the Roman legions essentially left to fight more urgent battles. Now in a weakened position, the Celts were gradually confined by the Germanic invaders to Wales, Scotland, and Cornwall, and to Ireland—this, in spite of a possible great battle won in about 450 C.E., in which the Celtic peoples were said to have been led by the legendary King Arthur of Camelot.

The Germanic peoples, first the Angles and Saxons (the Anglo-Saxons) and later their cousins the Norsemen or Vikings from Scandinavia, of course brought their own religious traditions and accompanying myths. The Germanic peoples, like the Romans and the Celts, were Indo-Europeans, a fact that explains a certain compatibility between Celtic, Roman, and Germanic mythology, and even with Romanized Christianity, which would achieve hegemony in the British Isles by the mid-seventh century C.E.

When discussing insular Celtic mythology, then, several factors need to be kept in mind. While it is true that druidic, brahmanlike bards or *filidh* kept the ancient stories alive, there was significant passage of time between the Celtic arrival in Britain and the compilation of the ancient sagas by Irish Christian monks in the sixth century C.E. and much later Welsh writers. And there is the peculiar mixture of traditions resulting from the contact in the British Isles between the cultures of indigenous peoples, the invading continental Celts, the Romans, the Germanic peoples, and the Christian missionaries. It can be argued, therefore, that Celtic-based mythology in the British Isles can be more reasonably referred to as Irish and Welsh rather than Celtic.

Irish Mythology

The first point to be made about Irish mythology, however, is
that although the form in which it comes down to us is in manuscripts written by Christian monks, linguistic evidence suggests
that the subject matter of those manuscripts was, in fact, reasonably well preserved from much earlier material. That is, the
monks were committed to their Christian point of view and
made certain Christian adaptations, but they were Irishmen,
clearly intent on preserving Irish culture. Furthermore, Irish-
Celtic culture had been less disrupted than that of the rest of the
British Isles by the arrival of Romans and Christians. Essentially,
Ireland escaped the Roman invasions, and Christianity seems to
have had minimal effect on the culture until after St. Patrick arrived there in the mid-fifth century. Finally, the hereditary *filidh*
continued to preserve and orally transmit the ancient stories well
after the establishment of Christianity.

The Irish mythological narratives were first written down in
the vernacular, adapted into the Latin alphabet, by monks in the
sixth century c.e. It can be argued, in fact, that by the middle of
the seventh century, all or most of what we now think of as Irish
mythology had been written down. The great *Tech Screpta* in which
the early manuscripts were kept, however, were gradually looted,
primarily by the Viking raiders of the late eighth century, and all
but fragments of the manuscripts were destroyed. Our primary
sources for Irish mythology are manuscripts written beginning in
the early twelfth century. The monks who wrote these manuscripts, like the earlier ones, clearly did so with the intention of
preserving the ancient traditions.

The earliest of the twelfth-century manuscripts is the *Lebhor na
hUidhre* (Book of the Dun Cow), on which the primary work has
traditionally been attributed to Mael Muire Mac Ceilchair, who
was killed in a raid at the monastery of Clonmacnois in about
1106. The so-called Rawlison Manuscript B 502 in the Bodleian

Library at Oxford, probably from the monastery at Glendalough or also from Clonmacnois, dates from about 1130. The *Lebhor na Nuachongbhála* or *Lebhor Laignech* (Book of Leinster) is said to have been compiled by Aed Mac Crimthainn at the monastery at Terryglass in about 1150. The next two hundred years or so saw the production of the Great Book of Lecan, the Yellow Book of Lecan, the Book of Ballymote, the Book of Lismore, and the Book of Fermoy, all based on much earlier texts. A particularly important source for Irish mythology, particularly the mythical history of Ireland, is a compilation known as the *Leabhor Gabhála Éireann* (the Book of the Taking of Ireland, or more commonly, the Book of Invasions) based on parts of various manuscripts, especially the Book of Leinster. The most complete version of this work is Michael O Cleirigh's, dating from the early seventeenth century. Also important are the various versions of the *Cath Maige Tuired* (the Battle of Mag Tuired or Magh Tuireadh), especially the somewhat later account known as the Second Battle of Mag Tuired.

Heroic mythology in Ireland centers around a cycle of tales known as the Ulster or Red Branch Cycle. The sources for these sagas are primarily the Book of the Dun Cow, the Book of Leinster, and the Yellow Book of Lecan, out of which emerge the great Irish epic narrative, the *Táin Bó Cuailnge* (the Cattle Raid of Cuailnge) and the lesser known *Táin Bó Fraoch* (the Cattle Raid of Fraoch). The twelfth century *Acallam na Senorach* (Colloquy of the Ancients) is the literary form of a series of heroic tales, some of them extremely ancient in origin, known as the Fenian or Ossianic cycle.

The Invasions

Central to Irish mythology is a mytho-historical version, derived from the many texts listed above, of the settlement of Ireland. There are conflicting versions of certain details in the story but the essential elements are consistent. The invasions begin, according to the Christian redactors, with the arrival of Noah's granddaughter Cesair (or of Banbha, one of the eponymous queens or symbols of Irish sovereignty) before the Flood. According to the Cesair myth, the Flood destroyed all of these first invaders except for Cesair's husband Fintan (the Ancient White One) who, according to some, saved himself by changing into a salmon. The myth claims that Fintan survived into the Christian period as a source of knowledge about the past.

Partholon and his people were the second invaders. Partholon developed social customs and traditions and began clearing land. But after fighting the simultaneously arriving Fomorians (Fomorii or Fomhoire), one-armed, one-legged, violent demons from under or beyond the sea, the Partholonians died of a plague.

Next came Nemed (Nemhedh) and his four women, the originators of the Nemedians, who also developed customs and crafts and cleared land. When Nemed was killed in battle with the Fomorians, his people were so mistreated by their conquerors that they revolted and emigrated to other lands. According to one version of the story, a group descending from the Nemedians returned to Ireland as the Firbolg (Fir Bholg) or "bag men"—so-named, say some, because, as slaves in distant Thrace, they had been made to carry bags of earth. The Firbolg, who could represent an actual pre-Celtic people in Ireland, are credited with the important division of the island into five provinces or *coiceds* (fifths) and with the establishment of a sacred kingship based on the relationship between the king's essential integrity and the land's fertility. The five provinces, which are basic to Irish myth and history, are Ulster in the north, Connaught in the west, Munster in the south, Leinster in the east, all held together by Mide (Meath), with Tara, the seat of the sacred king, at its center. The age of the Firbolg was a golden age of prosperity and peace.

The Irish Pantheon

The next invaders, the Tuatha Dé Danann (People of Danu), are the closest beings in Irish mythology to the deities of the great pantheons of the Indo-European tradition. Perhaps also descendants of the Nemedians, who in their time of exile—some say in the Northern Greek islands—learned the mysteries of creation, the Tuatha had, in one way or another, become deities by the time they arrived in Ireland. They brought with them great powers of magic and druidry, symbolized by four talismans: the Fal Stone, which cried out to announce the true king when he stood on it, Lugh's Spear of Victory, Nuada's (Nuadha or Nuadhu) Undefeatable Sword, and Dagda's (Daghdah or the Dagda) Never Empty Cauldron.

The Tuatha Dé Danann, as their name indicates, were descendants of the mother goddess Danu, of whom little is known. Their functions reflect a version of the Indo-European tripartite arrangement: sovereign/priest, warrior, and artisan. Many of the Tuatha have been associated with Romano-Celtic figures of the continent. Caesar's Mercury is the Irish Lugh, who contains the tripartite arrangement within himself. He is master of arts and crafts, a warrior, the source of divine kingship as druidic priest. As sometimes King of the Otherworld, he is enthroned with a queen representing sovereignty in Ireland. The Gaulish Apollo is related to the Irish Mac ind (Og), or Aonghus (Oenghus), son of the All Father Dagda (Good God in the sense of "good at everything") and known as a lover and a trickster. Dagda is the supreme representative of the priestly class, the supreme druid. Caesar's Minerva is reflected in aspects of Dagda's daughter Brigid (Brighid), a healer and patroness of crafts and learning, who would later be assimilated by Christians as St. Brigid of Kildare and perhaps, in another context, by the British as Briganytia and then Britannia. As Brigid of Kildare she was associated with sacred fire protected by many virgins, similar to the Vestal Virgins of Rome. In Scotland she was honored as the midwife of Mary and the foster mother of Jesus. The Vulcan of Gaul has a counterpart in Goibhniu, the smith god of Ireland. Dis Pater, the god of death in Gaul, has a counterpart in the mysterious Donn, the Brown One who can be associated with the great bull of the *Táin Bó Cuailnge*. The Irish Ogma (Oghma) is in all likelihood a cognate for the Roman Hercules. Other important figures among the Tuatha Dé Danaan are Dian Cecht the healer, King Nuada of the Silver Arm and his warrior queen Macha, who like so many Irish deities is a triune figure, first appears as the wife of Nemed and later emerges as the Queen of Ulster.

When the Tuatha arrived in Ireland and established their court at Tara, they fought and defeated the Firbolg in the first battle of Mag Tuired in which King Nuada lost his arm. Although the arm was replaced with a silver one by Dian Cecht and later with a real one by Dian Cecht's son Miach, Nuada abdicated his position as king because of his weakened condition when the Tuatha were faced with a new battle, this time against the Fomorians, who had returned to Ireland. Bres (the Beautiful One), the son of a Fomorian father and a Tuatha mother, was elected king, but when he proved so unsuitable as to elicit the satire of the poet Coibre—the voice of poets always carried great weight in Ireland—he was asked to resign. Instead he turned to his enemy relatives for support, and the second battle of Mag Tuired resulted.

Before the battle, Nuada was restored to the throne, but he soon ceded his power to Lugh, who came to Tara and proved his ability to call successfully upon magical powers. Lugh led the battle, finally facing the horrid Balar, who killed both Nuada and Queen Macha and whose dreadful one eye could destroy whole armies. With his slingstone, Lugh hit Balar's eye. The stone forced the eye back through the demon's skull and turned its evil powers against the Fomorians, who were themselves destroyed and removed from Ireland forever. Bres was captured but allowed to live in return for revealing Fomorian secrets of agriculture. Like the Norse Vanir, and the Greek and Vedic Giants against whom the gods must wage war, the Fomorians represented the powers of both fertility and destruction that exist together in nature.

The Celtic Invasion

The next mytho-historical invasion of Ireland is that of the Gaels or Irish Celts, represented by the Milesians or Sons of Mil (Mil Espaine or Mil of Spain). There are many stories of how the Milesians eventually came to Ireland, and the Christian monks who wrote the Book of Invasions gave this story of Irish origins a resemblance to the biblical Book of Exodus. The Milesians journeyed from Scythia to Egypt, to Spain, and eventually to Ireland where they landed, led by the poet Amairgen (Amhairghin) who used his Moses-like prophetic power and wisdom to push aside the defending cloud of mist arranged by Tuatha Dé Danaan on the Feast of Beltene (May Day). The poet in a sense sings the new Ireland of the Celts into existence, containing within himself, like Kṛṣṇa-Viṣṇu in the *Bhagavad Gītā* or the persona of the poems of Walt Whitman, all the elements of creation: "The sea's wind am I," he sings,

The ocean's wave,
The sea's roar,
The Bull of the Seven Fights,
The vulture on the cliff,
The drop of dew,
The fairest flower,
The boldest boar,
The salmon in the pool,
The lake on the plain,
The skillful word,

The weapon's point,
The god who makes fire I am,

 . . .

On their way to Tara the Milesians met the triune eponymous queens—Banba (Banbha), Fotla (Fodla), and Eire (Eriu), who convinced the invaders to preserve their names forever. At Tara they met with the three kings, Mac Cuill, Mac Cecht, and Mac Greine, who asked for a temporary truce. It was decided by Amairgen that the Milesians should put out to sea and invade again. The second invasion was prevented by the magic wind of the Tuatha until the stronger magic of the poet's words caused the Tuatha wind to fail. The Milesians then landed and were able to defeat the old gods. The peace settlement left the Celts in control of the world above ground and the Tuatha in control of the land below. The Tuatha were said from then on to live in sidhe, underground mounds, and were themselves referred to ever after as the *sidh*, the fairies or little people of Irish legends.

 Ireland was now ready for the heroic and tragic events surrounding the lives of the likes of Cuchulainn, Conchobhar, Fergus, Queen Medb (Medbh, Maeve), Finn, Oisin, Conaire and so many others, who will be treated in a later chapter. These events are described in such works as the *Táin* and the much later Fenian Cycle, the Irish equivalents of the Indian *Mahābhārata* and *Rāmāyaṇa*, the epics of the Germanic and Slavic peoples, and the more familiar epics of Homer.

The Christian Invasion

Tradition has it that St. Patrick arrived in Ireland in 432 C.E. to begin his conversion of the Irish to Christianity. Many myths are told in connection with Patrick. According to one such myth, the infant Patrick was brought to the blind Gornias to be baptized, but no water was available until Gornias used the child's hand to make the sign of the cross over the dry ground. Immediately water sprang up and Gornias was cured of his blindness and given the power to speak the baptizing formulas. Another myth tells of Patrick's arrival. As Amairgen and the Milesians had arrived in Ireland on the Feast of Beltene in ancient times to proclaim a Celtic Ireland, Patrick arrived on the Feast of Beltene to claim the land for his dying and risen god. Beltene refers to "bright fire" and druidic rites included purifying fires at Beltene. It is said that when Patrick arrived at Tara, he set a huge bonfire, thus undermining the druidic tradition. As divine Tuatha Dé Danann powers had overcome the Firbolg and Fomorians, and Amairgen's creation poetry had supplanted Tuatha magic, the spiritual fire of the Christian Holy Spirit, the source of this new invader's magic, would conquer the soul of Celtic Ireland.

Welsh Mythology

Welsh mythology has come to us from various sources, all more directly affected and distorted by time and non-Celtic elements than is the case in the much more isolated Ireland. There are the two Latin texts especially concerned with the Arthurian legends: the early ninth-century *Historia Brittonum* by Nennius and the twelfth-century *Historia regum Britanniae* by Geoffrey of Monmouth; and there are, of course, oral sources, including, traditionally, poems questionably attributed to the semimythic sixth-century poet-prophet Taliesen, whose Irish equivalent was Amairgen, the poet-warrior. But Welsh mythology, including the remnants of a pre-Christian Welsh pantheon, is more essentially contained in a collection of 11 medieval tales known in modern times as the *Mabinogion* (*Mabinogi*).

The *Mabinogion* is found in two fourteenth-century manuscripts, the *White Book of Rhydderch* and the *Red Book of Hergest*. The collection, based on oral narratives, probably took literary form between the mid-eleventh to the early twelfth centuries.

There are, for instance, parts of what seem originally to have been mid-eleventh century written versions of a few tales in an early thirteenth-century manuscript known as *Peniarth 6*. The primary mythological material of the *Mabinogion* is contained in the four sections known as the Four Branches. Also included in the greater *Mabinogion* are the four "Independent Native Tales," so named by Lady Charlotte Elizabeth Guest, the first to translate the Welsh stories into English. This group includes the earliest known Welsh Arthurian story, "Culhwch and Olwen." The last part of the *Mabinogion* is made up of three later Arthurian romances.

The term *mabinogi* has been associated with the tradition of the *mabinog*, or young apprentice bard, and with the Irish *Mac ind oc*, a name sometimes given to the god Dagda's son Aonghus (the son of the eternal youth). As the Four Branches are concerned with the children of Don, who resemble the Irish Tuatha de Danann, this theory seems at least reasonable, especially since the only character to figure in all four tales is Pryderi, who in Wales was always the *Mac ind Og*. Finally, *mabinogi* has been associated with Maponos, the divine youth god popular in northern Britain and the continent, who is the Arthurian warrior and hunter Mabon in Wales. Thus, the theory goes, *mabinogi* is derived from Mabonalia. The mother of Maponos was the mother goddess Matrona; in Wales she became Madron. In some stories we learn that Mabon was stolen from his mother soon after his birth. This theme occurs, as will be seen, in other Welsh tales as well.

The Four Branches of the *Mabinogion*

The Four Branches are independent narratives that are, however, related, as certain characters appear in more than one tale. Only Pryderi, whose birth story is the subject of part of the First Branch, appears in all four. (Much of the following retelling of the *Mabinogion* is taken from Christopher Fee with David Leeming, *Gods, Heroes, and Kings: the Battle for Mythic Britain*, 181–9).

The First Branch

Pryderi was the son of Pwyll (Good Judgment), lord of Dyfed, and Rhiannon. Dyfed was the land of the Cauldron of Plenty (perhaps the Holy Grail), and in this context Pwyll is the Arthurian Pelles, the guardian of the Grail. He was also known as "head of Annwn."

While hunting in Glyn Cuch, Pwyll insults another hunter, who turns out to be the mysterious King Arawn of the Otherworld realm called Annwn (Annwfn). Pwyll's offense is driving away the king's hounds and substituting his own in the pursuit of a stag. To pay for his discourtesy, he is made to take Arawn's face and to occupy his throne in Annwn for a year. There he sleeps in Arawn's bed, keeping a promise not to make love with his wife, and he defeats the king's enemy Hafgan, another Otherworld king. Pwyll wins the fight with Hafgan only by restraining himself from administering a second blow, which would have restored power to his enemy.

Soon after his return to Dyfed, in southwestern Wales, Pwyll holds a feast at his court, Arbeth. He takes his place on the throne mound knowing full well that by so doing he will suffer pain or bear witness to something wonderful. A beautiful woman rides by on a white horse. After a fruitless chase of the woman, Pwyll begs her to stop, which she does. The woman reveals herself to be Rhiannon, and she offers herself as Pwyll's wife. Rhiannon is possibly the Welsh form of the Irish goddesses Edain Echraide (horse riding) and Macha, who outran horses. All are figures comparable to Matrona and to the horse goddess Epona, whose legacy stretches back to early Indo-European horse-based myths and rituals mentioned earlier.

At the wedding feast a year later, Pwyll foolishly grants a wish that results in his losing Rhiannon to Gwawl (Light), the son of the goddess Clud. But Pwyll wins his wife back at the wedding feast of Gwawl and Rhiannon. Rhiannon has given him a magic bag, which he tricks Gwawl into entering. Once there Gwawl is badly kicked and beaten by Pwyll's followers, who thus originate the game called badger the bag.

After three years of marriage, Rhiannon gives birth to Pryderi. The women who are supposed to watch over the mother and child, fall asleep, and the baby is mysteriously abducted, reminding us of the story of Mabon's similar abduction. To save themselves, the women smear the blood of some killed puppies on Rhiannon so that she is accused of killing her child and is wrongly punished by her husband.

After several years, the child is discovered to be alive and safe in the home of Teyrnon of Gwent and Is-Coed and is returned to his parents. The child has been named Gwri, or Golden Hair, but Rhiannon, relieved of her worry—her care—renames him Pryderi, or Care.

It seems that Teyrnon had amputated a giant clawed arm that had reached through a stable window on May Eve to take one of his foals. He had rushed out to give chase to the intruder but had found no one. On his return to the stable, he had found a baby, and he and his wife had raised the boy, who turned out to be the lost son of Pwyll and Rhiannon.

The Second Branch

The Second Branch of the *Mabinogion* concerns the Children of Llyr (Irish Lir—perhaps King Lear), the gigantic Bran the Blessed, King of Britain, the gentle Branwen, sometimes thought of as a goddess of love, Manawydan, the sea god, and their half brothers, Efnisien, the bringer of strife, and Nisien, the peacemaker. Efnisien is responsible for much of the tragedy in the story of Branwen's marriage to King Matholwch of Ireland. According to some sources, Llyr's first wife was Iweriadd, or Ireland, and she was the mother of Bran and Branwen. According to others, it was his wife Penardun, the daughter of the mother goddess Don, who was the mother of Bran and Branwen and certainly of Manawydan. She is also the mother of Efnisien and Nisien by a later husband, Eurosswyd.

Matholwc comes to Harlech in Wales to ask for Branwen in marriage. All goes well at the marriage feast in Aberffraw until Efnisien, angry at not being a part of the marriage arrangements, damages Matholwc's horses. To cool the bridegroom's anger, Bran gives his brother-in-law a magic cauldron—perhaps the Cauldron of Plenty—which will bring the wounded back to life but leave them without the power of speech.

During her first year in Ireland, Branwen gives birth to a son who is named Gwern, on whom the "sovranty" of Ireland is bestowed so as to bring lasting peace between Bran and Matholwc. But the people of Ireland continue to be outraged by the behavior of Efnisien at the marriage feast in Wales, and they demand that Branwen be made to suffer. So for three years she is made to work in the court kitchens and to experience the daily blows of the court butcher.

Branwen teaches a starling to speak, however, and it takes a message to her brother concerning her misery. Bran invades Ireland, his gigantic body forming a bridge between the lands by which his army can pass into Ireland. We are reminded here of the exploits of the monkey god Hanumān in the Indian epic the *Rāmāyaṇa*, when the god-hero Rāmā invades Ceylon to free his captured wife Sītā.

Matholwch sues for peace to save his country, but Efnisien destroys the truce by hurling Gwern into a fire. A terrible battle ensues in which Efnisien sacrifices himself and in so doing destroys the magic cauldron which is constantly causing the resuscitation of the Irish. Bran is wounded by a poison arrow and orders his followers to cut off his head and to return it to Britain. The severed head goes on talking and eating during a long and difficult voyage back to Britain. The prominent Celtic theme of decapitation and the talking severed head suggests a belief that the soul resides in the head and lives on after death.

Very few people survive the great war, as in the case of the Irish second battle of Mag Tuired. Five pregnant women only remain alive in Ireland and are the source for that island's future population. The only survivors from Bran's forces include Manawydan, Pryderi, Taliesen, and four others. Branwen also survives and returns to Britain with these other survivors; soon after she dies of a broken heart over the destruction for which she blames herself. She is buried along the Alaw in Anglesey. The river is renamed Ynys Branwen.

The Third Branch

Pryderi has now married Cigva (Cigfa) and succeeded his late father Pwyll as Lord of Dyfed. His mother, Rhiannon, marries the wise and patient Manawydan, a surviving son of Llyr. Manawydan plays the major role in the Third Branch. Clearly he is a descendant of an earlier Celtic sea deity and a close relative of the benevolent Irish sea god who came from the Isle of Man. As the Irish Manannan mac Lir, he is associated with rebirth, serving as lord of the land of eternal youth.

During a feast at Arbeth, the two couples sit on the magic throne mound and are covered by a mysterious mist following a huge clap of thunder. When the mist clears, they find themselves in a land empty of living things. They wander about the deserted Dyfed for two years and then go to the land of Lloegyr (England), where Pryderi and Manawydan work as saddlers, shoemakers, and shieldmakers.

The four return to Arbeth, and the impulsive Pryderi, disregarding the advice of Manawydan, allows himself to be enticed by a magic boar into an enchanted castle containing a fountain in which a golden bowl sits on a marble slab. This is perhaps the Cauldron of Plenty. When Pryderi tries to grasp the cauldron, he loses speech and cannot release his hands from it. When Rhiannon tries to rescue her son, she, too, loses speech and the ability to release the cup. The two now disappear into a mist.

The author of the enchantment and abduction of the hero and his mother is Llwyd, a friend of the evil Gwawl, who had once attempted to marry Rhiannon through trickery.

Manawydan, accompanied by Cigva, returns to shoemaking in England but eventually goes back to Arbeth, where he grows corn. Having discovered an army of mice carrying away the corn, he captures the slowest moving of the army and is about to hang it as a thief on the throne mound when a bishop turns up and announces that the mouse is the bishop's pregnant wife. He reveals himself as Llwyd. In return for his wife's life, Llwyd ends forever the spells suffered by the heroic family.

The Fourth Branch

The Fourth Branch of the *Mabinogion* is dominated by the family of Don, especially Lleu, who resembles the Irish god Lugh. The tale begins with Math of Gwynedd, son of Mathonwy. Mathonwy was also the father of Don, the Welsh equivalent of the Irish Danu and the mother goddess of the House of Don. Math is a god of wealth and is possibly a cognate of the Irish Mathu. He is best known for the story of his requiring that his feet be held in the lap of a virgin when he is not at war. It is the ruse of two of the sons of Don, the magicians Gwydion and Gilfaethy, that deprives him of his footstool. Gwydion also dupes Pryderi in this process and the result is his death in a war against Gwynedd.

Gwydion attempts to substitute his sister Aranrhod for the stolen maiden. But Aranrhod drops a male child as she steps over Math's sword in a test of her virginity. And soon after the birth of the first child, the sea god Dylan, she drops an object which Gwydion takes and hides in a box, only to discover there later another child who is actually the incestuous offspring of Aranrhod and Gwydion. Aranrhod is ashamed and refuses to name the child but Gwydion and the child appear in court as shoemakers, and Aranrhod inadvertently names him by exclaiming over his brightness and skill. Thus he becomes Lleu Llawgyffes. Now the boy's mother swears that he will never bear arms unless she gives them to him, but Gwydion's magic overcomes this oath. Aranrhod also swears that Lleu will never marry into a race "now on earth," so Math and Gwydion create a woman, Blodeuwedd (Flower) from the blossoms of the oak, the broom, and the meadowsweet, and she becomes Lleu's wife.

Blodeuwedd falls in love with Gronw Pebyr of Penllyn, however, and the lovers plot to kill Lleu. Like many *femmes fatales* before and after her, Blodeuwedd convinces her husband to reveal his particular weakness and learns that he can never be killed in a house or on horseback or on foot outside. Only a specially created spear can kill him. So one day when Lleu is taking a bath, he is tricked into standing with one foot on the tub and the other on a goat. In this position he is vulnerable and falls victim to Gronw's spear. He disappears as an eagle but is found by Gwydion, who gives him back his human form. Lleu returns to Gwynedd and kills Gronw. Blodeuwedd is turned into the despised owl.

Four Independent Native Tales

The Four Independent Tales are a combination of folk history and popular themes and lack the narrative depth of the Four Branches.

Macsen Wledig

The first tale, Macsen Wledig, sometimes called the Dream of Macsen, concerns Magnus Maximus, a Spanish Roman who came to Britain in 368 C.E. and married Helen, or Elen Lwddog. In 383 he proclaimed himself Western Emperor, crossed over into Gaul and attacked Rome. Defeated by the Eastern Emperor

Theodosius, he was put to death in 388. Elen returned to Britain and settled in what would become Wales with her children, whose offspring would be kings. The Dream of Macsen tells the story of Macsen's hunt, on which he was joined by 32 other kings, reminding us of a similar Irish story, Bricriu's Feast, in which Conchobhar is accompanied by 32 heroes to Bricriu's Hall. The number 33 is important in Indo-European mythology in general; there are, for instance, 33 gods mentioned in the Vedas.

Cyfranc Lludd a Llefelys

The story of Lludd and Llefelys, the second tale, is based on a Welsh translation by Geoffrey of Monmouth in the *Historia regum Britanniae* in the twelfth century C.E. Lludd (Nudd) and Llefelys were sons of Beli, the husband of Don. With the help of the wise counsel of his brother, King Lludd of Britain puts an end to three plagues that devastated Britain. The first plague was caused by the highly knowledgeable little Coraniaids, the second by the hideous scream of a British dragon fighting a foreign dragon under the very center of Britain on May Eve. It is probably more than coincidental that it was also on May Eve that Teyrnon amputated the mysterious invasive claw in the First Branch of the *Mabinogion*. In any case, the dragon scream undermined fertility all over the land. The third plague was brought about by a giant who ate prodigious amounts of food. These plagues bear some resemblance to those that the Fomorians in Ireland levied on the Tuatha de Danaan and to the mysterious events that took place in Pryderi's Dyfed. The story is full of the fantasy of fairy tale. Some have suggested that it is a popular account of mythological invasions of Britain.

Culhwch and Olwen

Dating from the mid-eleventh century, the third tale, that of Culwhch (Kulhwch) and Olwen, is based on several traditional folk tales and is the earliest Arthurian story in Welsh. Culhwch was the son of Cilydd and Goleuddydd, who lost her mind and ran into the woods and gave birth to Culwhch. Realizing she was about to die, she made her husband promise not to marry again until a two-headed briar grew from her grave. Cilydd respected his wife's wishes and waited the seven years until the briar grew as indicated before he married again.

The new wife hated Culhwch and put a curse on him because he refused to marry her daughter. The youth would never marry unless with Olwen, the daughter of Yspaddaden Pencawr (Benkawr), a terrifying giant. Olwen resembles Etain in Irish mythology; she is said to be so beautiful that white flowers spring up in her tracks as she walks.

Culhwch goes to his cousin King Arthur's court to learn the arts of knighthood and to discover the whereabouts of Olwen. Stopped at the king's door, he bursts into Arthur's hall on horseback, asks that Arthur perform on him the initiatory rite of cutting his hair and that the king obtain Olwen for him. He asks these favors in the name of a host of Welsh heroes. Arthur agrees to help, sends out scouts to find Olwen, and when that fails, Culhwch goes with several knights to find Olwen himself.

One day the party comes upon a castle where they meet a shepherd named Custennin, who is Yspaddaden's brother and whose wife is Culwhch's mother's sister. The couple bring Olwen to meet Culhwch, and the hero asks the beautiful maiden to marry him. Olwen will only agree to the marriage if her father consents as, according to a prophecy, he will die when his daughter marries.

Culhwch and his companions enter the castle, where servants hold open the giant's eyes with forks so that he can see his visitors. Culwhch asks for Olwen's hand in marriage, and the giant agrees to consider the matter, but as the knights are leaving he hurls a spear at them. Bedwyr catches it and hurls it back, wounding Yspaddaden in the knee. The same thing happens the next day and the next, causing wounds to the giant's chest and to one of his eyes.

Finally, Yspaddaden agrees to the marriage if the hero can complete thirteen tasks. The tasks, reminiscent of those of Herakles and of the world of fairy tales, are, in effect, preparations for the marriage feast that the giant hopes to prevent. Culhwch must clear a forest and prepare the land for the growing of food for the wedding feast, he must find linseed for the flax that will be used for his wife's veil, he must find perfect honey for the wedding drink, the magic cup of Llwyr to contain it, and four other magical vessels, including the famous Irish cauldron of Diwrnach for the cooking of the meat. He must even obtain a magical harp and the birds of Rhiannon so that there will be music at the feast. And he must take a tusk from Yskithyrwyn, the head boar, to serve as Ysbaddaden's razor, the Black Witch's blood as lotion for his beard. And for the giant's hair management, he must take scissors and a comb from between the ears of Twrch Trwyth, a king who has been turned into a boar. All of these tasks and some 26 additional ones are accomplished with the help of the Arthurian knights, various animals, and even some gods, including Gofannon son of Don, Gwynn son of (Lludd) Nudd, and Mabon (Maponos) son of Modron, whom Culhwch rescues from the Otherworld, Caer Loyw. Finally Yspaddaden concedes defeat and is decapitated according to the Celtic practice we have encountered earlier, leaving Culhwch and Olwen free to marry.

The Dream of Rhonabwy

Probably dating from the thirteenth century, the Dream of Rhonabwy, the fourth tale, takes place in the context of a rebellion by Iorwerth against his brother Madawc, son of Maredudd. It is Rhonabwy who leads Madawc's troops and who one evening falls asleep on a calf's hide and remains sleeping for three nights, dreaming of King Arthur's game of chess with Owain, who has an army of 300 ravens, and of the gathering of Arthur's forces for the great sixth-century Battle of Mount Badon, in which the Celts defeated the Anglo-Saxons.

The Later Arthurian Tales

The three late Arthurian tales of the *Mabinogion* are derived from twelfth-century romances of the French poet Chrétien de Troyes whose sources seem to have been earlier Welsh and/or Breton versions. The theme that unites them is that of valid sovereignty and specifically the idea we have found to be so prevalent in Irish mythology that agricultural fertility depends on the marriage of the king or hero to a goddess who represents the land in question.

Owein or the Lady of the Fountain

Owein (Owain), son of Urien, is one of King Arthur's most trusted knights. We remember that in the Dream of Rhonabwy he plays a game of chess with the king, a game which, in a sense, can be seen as a preface to the story of his connection with the Lady of the Fountain.

After he defeats the Black Knight, Owein finds himself a prisoner in the Castle of the Fountain until he is rescued by a ring of invisibility given to him by a beautiful young woman named Luned. Luned instructs him on how to win the love of the Lady of the Fountain, which he succeeds in doing before returning to Arthur's court. There he forgets the lady until she appears and accuses him of being a faithless knight.

Embarrassed and ashamed, Owein escapes to the wilderness where he is saved from death by the ministrations of a noblewoman and her assistants. After killing two monstrous beasts, he saves Luned and 24 maidens, whom he finds imprisoned by the Black Giant. He is now worthy of the Lady of the Fountain, whom he marries.

Peredur, Son of Efrawk

The seventh son of Efrawk (Efrawg), Peredur is the Welsh version and apparent source for the hero Percival, or Parzifal. The best known versions of his story are Chrétien's late twelfth-century *Percival, ou le conte du Graal* and Sir Thomas Malory's fifteenth-century *Le Morte d'Arthur*, where he is also Percival. *Per* means bowl in Brythonic Celtic, and Peredur-Percival-Parzival is always a hero who searches for the bowl that is the holy grail. In all of the tales the hero has a rough beginning, living an unmannered, unschooled life in the woods, until he arrives at Arthur's court, behaves in a bumbling sort of way, but is trained as a knight. Perhaps it is Peredur's essential innocence—even naiveté, which makes it possible for him to see the holy grail itself. Or perhaps his fortune is guaranteed by the young maiden relative who repeatedly guides him to the right path.

Gereint and Enid

The story of Gereint (Geraint) and Enid is a romance about a lover—perhaps based on a king of Dumnonia (the Celtic area of western Britain in early Anglo-Saxon times)—who has little faith in the constancy of his beloved, Enid, the chieftain's daughter later to be made famous in the Tennyson poem named for her. Because of his doubts, Gereint treats Enid with contempt, but she proves herself in several tests, and eventually the two are reconciled, once again bringing the hero into proper relationship with the representative of sovereignty.

The Arthurian Legacy and Christianity

As St. Patrick and the stories surrounding him represent the coming of Christianity to Ireland, similarly the Arthurian story gradually became a central aspect of the whole Christian mythological system as it applied specifically to Great Britain. Con-

nected with the Arthurian myth, for instance, is the story of
Joseph of Arimathea, who provided the burial place for Jesus
after his crucifixion (Luke 23), and who, according to tradition,
traveled to England after Jesus' resurrection, bringing with him
the holy grail (Sangreale), the vessel used by Jesus at the Last
Supper. The grail would be the goal of the quest of the Arthurian knights and the symbol of the Christian quest in general.
Joseph was said to have been responsible for the building of the
church at Glastonbury, where his staff gave forth the holy thorn
tree that is still there. And the monks at the great abbey at Glastonbury claim King Arthur was buried there.

The tradition of Joseph's journey to England is related in
spirit to the tradition that Jesus himself came to Britain after the
resurrection, a tradition forming the basis for William Blake's
words to the hymn "Jerusalem," arguably the spiritual national
anthem of Great Britain:

> And did those feet in ancient time
> Walk upon England's mountains green?
> And was the holy Lamb of God
> On England's pleasant pastures seen?
>
> And did the Countenance Divine
> Shine forth upon our clouded hills?
> And was Jerusalem builded here
> Among these dark Satanic Mills?
>
> Bring me my Bow of burning gold:
> Bring me my Arrows of Desire:
> Bring me my Spear: O clouds unfold!
> Bring me my Chariot of Fire.
>
> I will not cease from Mental Fight,
> Nor shall my Sword sleep in my hand

Til we have built Jerusalem
In England's green and pleasant Land.
("Prelude" from "Milton")

At the fringes of all of this national mythology is the Arthurian Fisher King, whose wounds must be cured before Britain can cease to be a wasteland. And not far from this myth and the Christian story is that of the once and future king himself, a myth that will be treated in detail in a later chapter.

6

Germanic Mythology

THE TERM GERMANIC mythology refers to the gods and heroes of European peoples that include Germans, Scandinavians, and Anglo-Saxons. These are people whose languages—one of which would evolve into Old English and then, with other influences, into Middle and Modern English—derive from the same Indo-European branch. Terms commonly applied to the most northern of the Germanic peoples are Norse and, during the ninth, tenth, and eleventh centuries, Viking. Germanic mythology has a certain unity of theme and narrative but reflects the conditions of several cultures "contaminated" in various degrees by surrounding realities. Thus, the Anglo-Saxon epic *Beowulf* in Old English contains elements of Germanic mythology, as do the later German epic the *Nibelungenlied*, the Scandinavian *Völsunga Saga*, and especially the *Eddas* of Iceland. But all these works bear the marks and influences of the Christian era in which they took literary form.

The Germanic People and the Romans

The Germanic people emerged in the early Iron Age "Jastorf" culture in what is now Scandinavia and northern Germany at the beginning of the sixth century B.C.E., although Bronze Age rock carvings in Scandinavia suggest a much earlier birth (Crossley-Holland, xxxII). Like their early neighbors the Celts, the Germanic peoples did not possess a written language beyond the eventual development of a limited runic script until after their gradual Christianization in the Middle Ages. In fact, the first lengthy work in a Germanic language is a fourth-century C.E. Gothic-Visigoth translation of the Bible. The early Germans, who were herders and rudimentary agriculturalists, were thought of as barbarians by the Romans. Most of what we know of them comes from the writings of Julius Caesar and especially the Roman historian Tacitus, who in his *Germania* provides, as in the case of Caesar and the Celts, a highly Romanized version of the Germanic gods. Occasional Germanic forays into Gaul such as one undertaken by Teutones and Cimbris in 101 B.C.E. were crushed by Roman legions. Later the Romans were not so successful against the Germans, being defeated by them, for instance, in the Teutoburgerwald in 9 C.E. And with the general weakening of Rome, Germanic peoples moved into lands formerly protected by the great empire. In 167 C.E. Germanic tribes swept into northern Italy and soon after into Spain, Gaul, and Africa. In 380, Visigoths led by Alaric sacked Rome itself. By the end of the so-called migration period of the fourth and fifth centuries C.E., Germanic peoples were dominant in much of Europe. Franks were in what is now France; Jutes, Angles, and Saxons had pushed Celts to the fringes of Britain; and in 800 Charlemagne, a Germanic Frank, was crowned Holy Roman Emperor.

By the end of the sixth century most of the Germanic peoples, including the Anglo-Saxons of Britain, had adopted Christianity, a fact that combined with the lack of writing leaves us with limited firsthand knowledge of Germanic mythology. Works like the Anglo-Saxon *Beowulf* and the German *Nibelungenlied* are products of Christianized writers. The German epic is particularly contaminated by Christian and classical influences. Christianity was slow to achieve hegemony in Scandinavia, however, and it is the so-called Viking Age there that provides most of the material for later redactions of Germanic mythology.

The Vikings

Vikings, or Norsemen, were Swedes, Danes, and Norwegians who between 780 and 1070 undertook wide-scale raids and in many cases colonization in what was, in effect, a second migration period for Germanic peoples. Vikings took much of the British Isles, found their way to Italy, Spain, and Southern France, and to Kiev, Constantinople, and Baghdad in the east, and probably to pre-Columbian North America in the west. Most important for the student of Germanic mythology, they colonized Iceland, where, in a somewhat isolated situation, there developed what Jaan Puhvel calls "a flowering of antiquarian culture" (190).

It was not until the year 1000 that the Icelandic Assembly voted to give up the old religion in favor of Christianity, and the old gods remained supreme in Sweden for longer than that. The eleventh-century German historian Adam of Bremen and many others reported eyewitness accounts of sacrifices to Odin at the great temple in Uppsala as late as 1070. All of this was several centuries after the British Isles and the Germans and other peoples south of Scandinavia had become Christian.

The Icelandic historian Snorri Sturluson (1179–1241) and the Danish historian Saxo Grammaticus (1150–1216)—two of our most important redactors of Germanic or Norse mythology— were, therefore, several centuries closer to their material than was, for instance, the author of the *Nibelungenlied* in Germany. Like the writing monks of Ireland, Saxo and especially Snorri had a genuine desire to preserve knowledge of an ancient culture that, although relatively recent, was no longer a threat to contemporary beliefs. Saxo wrote in Latin but with real knowledge of the Norse sagas. His *Gesta Danorum* (History of the Danes) corroborates much of the more extensive work of Snorri.

Snorri, the Eddas, and Norse Mytholgy

It is on the Icelander Snorri Sturluson and his sources that we depend most for our knowledge of Germanic or Norse mythology. In 1643 in an old Icelandic farmhouse, the bishop of Skalholt found a manuscript, the *Codex Regius*, containing a collection of probably pre-Christian mythical poems of the Viking period, only written down, however, in the late thirteenth century. Traditionally, the compilation of these poems has been attributed to Saemund Sigfusson and thus called *Saemund's Edda* (*Edda* in all likelihood coming from a word meaning poetry). A few other mythological poems were discovered soon after the *Codex Regius*, and the whole collection is known more commonly as the *Elder Edda* or simply the *Poetic Edda*, within which the most famous poems and the ones most used by Snorri are *Voluspa* (the Prophecy of the Seeress), containing the great story of the beginning and end of the world; *Grimnismal*, in which the high god Odin speaks in disguise as Grimnir (the Hooded One); and *Havamal*, which contains the story of the self-hanging of the high god Odin. Other poetic sources for Snorri and later mythologists and historians are the highly alliterative skaldic poems (*skalds* were bards, the *filidh* of the north), known in literary circles for their extensive use of kennings (namings), compound metaphorical substitutions for the names of things (for example, "whale-road" for the sea, "Freya's tears" for gold). The skaldic form was common in Old English poetry as well as in the Old Norse.

For his work, Snorri depended on his knowledge of Eddic and skaldic poetry and on his own talent as a saga writer, poet, historian, and antiquarian. His mission was to encourage Icelandic poets not to lose sight of the stories and methods of skaldic and Eddic poetry. Snorri himself wrote skaldic poetry, as in *Hattatal*, a eulogy for two noblemen, and sagas based on the Icelandic sagas (the *Fornaldar Sogur*). Snorri's *Heimskringla*, compiled from poems and sagas, is a history of Norwegian kings from mythical time until 1177 and contains *Ynglingasaga*, an important source for Norse mythology, tracing the pre-Norwegian Swedish kings and their mythological ancestors back to the god Odin.

By far, Snorri's most important work, however, is his *Edda*, or *Prose Edda*, as it is called to differentiate it from the *Poetic Edda*. In particularly beautiful Icelandic prose, Snorri retold the stories gleaned from his scholarship in the Eddic and skaldic poetry and the old sagas. Written in about 1220, his *Edda* was intended to be a handbook and guide to the old mythology for poets and scholars. The *Prose Edda* begins with an introduction called the *Gylfaginning* (the Deluding of Gylfi), in which a fictional Swedish king, Gylfi, disguised as a beggar called Gangleri, visits Asgard, the home of the gods, and questions the also-disguised Odin (Wotan in Germany) and two other mysterious figures about the ancient gods and mythological history. The second section of the *Prose Edda* is *Skaldskaparmal* (Poetic Diction), which supplies rules for traditional poetry and many myths as well. The final section is *Hattatal*, the eulogy-list in verse form mentioned above.

The Norse Cosmology

More than any other European or Indo-European mythology, Germanic mythology of the Norse tradition is in tune with the ancient Indian sense of life—including that of the gods—as being part of a larger process of creation, preservation, and destruction. For many this is an essentially pessimistic mythology, reflecting the long dark days of the seemingly endless northern winters. Others might see it in the Indian way, as the natural history of birth, death, and rebirth in the cosmic context.

The mythological universe of the Norsemen as depicted by

the *Poetic Edda* and Snorri's *Edda* was made up of three levels divided by space. The top level was Asgard, where the Aesir, the race of warrior gods led by Odin and Thor, lived. Here was the great hall Valhalla where slain warriors fought, were killed heroically again, but revived to feast on pork and mead. It was the Valkyries, Odin's maids, who summoned the warriors to Valhalla and who served them there. The warriors would fight in the great battle at the end of time. On this top level also lived the Vanir, the fertility gods who played the role of antagonists to the Aesir in one of the Norse versions of the Indo-European war in heaven. Eventually the Aesir and the Vanir would unite into one pantheon. Elves also lived on the top level of the universe, in Alfheim, and a place called Gimli housed the righteous dead.

Midgard, the world of humans, was the middle level of the universe. This was a world surrounded by a vast ocean containing the world serpent Jormungand who, according to Snorri, bit his own tail, thus forming a firm belt to hold the world together. The giants, the ultimate foes of the Aesir, lived either across the ocean or in another part of Midgard, a place called Jotunheim, protected by the fortress of the outer world, Utgard. Dwarfs dark elves lived in Nidavellir (Dark Home) and Svartalfheim in the north.

The lowest level of the universe contained Niflheim, the home of the wicked dead—a place of utter darkness with a citadel called Hel ruled over by a monstrous queen also named Hel, just, as the Greek Hades was a place ruled over by a god of the same name.

The axis of all three worlds was the great world tree Yggdrasill—the cosmic ash with roots leading to Hel and to the worlds of humans and the frost giants. At the foot of the tree were various springs and/or wells, depending on our source. Among these were the spring of Uror, the goddess of fate, and the well of Mimir (Wisdom).

The Germanic Pantheon

In the sixth book of the *Gallic Wars* Julius Caesar spoke of a Germanic cult of the sun and fire, reminding us of other Indo-European solar and fire deities—Mitra, Sürya, and Agni in Vedic India, Mithra in Iran, Apollo in Greece. At the end of the first century C.E. Tacitus outlined a pantheon following the typically Roman tendency to assimilate Roman religion with that of the enemy or conquered people. Tacitus called the primary god Mercury, a name associated with the Germanic Wodanaz or Wodan/Wotan (related to the Anglo-Saxon battle god Woden and later the Norse Odin): thus, the Latin *Mercurii dies*, the Germanic *Wodaniztag*, and the English *Wednesday* (Polome, 5:531). Following the Indo-European tripartite custom, Mercury is associated with two other gods, Mars—the Germanic Tiwaz or Tiw (Tig for the Anglo-Saxons, Tyr among the Old Norse)—and Herakles—the Germanic Thunaraz or Thunr (the Anglo-Saxon Thunor and later the Norse Thor): thus, *Martis dies* and the Old English *Tiwesdaeg* and our *Tuesday*; as the Romans also saw the Germanic Mars as Jupiter or Jove, the Latin *Jovis dies* but the Old Germanic *Thnrizdag*, and our *Thursday* (see Polome, 5:531). It seems likely that this god had once been the primary Germanic god and he would later be the most popular god in the Viking north.

Tacitus also speaks of several Germanic tribes having descended from Mannus, a kind of first man in the tradition of the Indian Manu and the Purusa, who like the Norse Ymir is the sacrificial victim out of which the world is born. Tacitus tells of the earth goddess Nerthus, too, one of the sacred *matres* or *matronae*, and the Twins or Alhiz. Both earth mothers and divine twins are, of course, basic to the overall Indo-European pantheon (e.g., the mother goddesses Matrona and Danu among the Celts, the *Discouri* in Greece, Romulus and Remus in Rome, the Aśvins in India).

During the migration period, Wodan remains the high god

and has clearly taken on the magical poetic and ecstatic qualities later associated with the Norse Odin. Like the Indic Rudra-Siva, who is both meditative yogi and destroyer, he is at least two-sided and similarly demands sacrifice. Thunr, in the meantime, becomes more clearly defined as a war god. Jaan Puhvel suggests that the Germanic Thunr and the Norse Thor took on qualities of the trustworthy warrior who balanced the volatile Odin, as in India Viṣṇu balances Śiva (201). Tiwaz, the third figure in the old Germanic tripartite structure seems to lose importance during the migration period, and fertility figures such as Friia (Anglo-Saxon Frig and Norse Frigg thus, *Friday*) seem to gain in importance.

Aesir vs. Vanir

But, again, it is to the Scandinavian or Norse world of the Viking age and specifically to the *Eddas* that we must look to find the full revelation of the Germanic pantheon. Snorri tells us that there were twelve primary gods and thirteen goddesses under Odin, the "Allfather," and his consort Frigg. Originally there had been two races of gods: warrior gods led by Odin and Thor called the Aesir, and fertility gods called the Vanir, the most famous of whom were Njord, Freyr, and the goddess Freyja.

The Vanir, as deities of the fertile earth, were closer to humans than the sky gods of Asgard. Their concern was not social order or morality but the productivity of earth and its inhabitants. Goddesses and sexuality—even orgies—were important to ancient worshippers of the Vanir, and we can assume, as Hilda Ellis Davidson suggests, that "Behind the goddesses of the Vanir is the conception of the Earth Mother, the Great Goddess who gives shelter to us all" (*Gods*, 126–7).

The Aesir were more to be feared. They were war gods and gods of social order, morality, and magic. The war between these two races of gods was as inevitable as other Indo-European wars between deities—for example, the war between the Tuatha and the Firbolg—and may be a distant metaphor for ancient clashes between pre-Indo-European peoples and their Indo-European warrior invaders. A later, more devastating war would be those between the giants and the gods at Ragnarok, the end of the world. Again, the Armageddon-like battles are fought in other Indo-European mythologies, as, for example, between the demons and gods of India and reflected in the human battle of the *Mahābhārata*, and between the Titans and Olympians in ancient Greece or the Tuatha Dé Danann and the Fomorians in Ireland.

The eventual truce between the Aesir and Vanir resulted in a valuable combination for gods and humans, based on the attributes of both races. Specifically it gave rise to the powers of the imagination, or inspiration, something akin to the Vedic word-power of ancient India, the poetic powers of the Celtic Amairgen and Taliesen, or the necessary ecstatic Dionysian and orderly Apollonian combination in the art of ancient Greece, and perhaps all art.

A strange myth explains the powers that were born of the joining of Aesir and Vanir. To confirm their truce, the Aesir and Vanir spat into a pot and out of the pot sprang Kvasir, the wisest of beings, who could answer any question. Soon Kvasir was made to play the role of sacrificial victim out of which new life would come. He was killed by two dwarfs, who mixed his blood with honey in two cauldrons. *Kvas* denotes an alcoholic beverage and, in keeping with the process of fermentation, the resulting liquid became a kind of mead; to drink it brought the magical fermentation we know as poetic imagination. But the mead was stolen by giants, as the Vedic *soma* had been stolen. In both ancient Indian and Norse myths the precious drink is recovered by the gods—in the Norse case by Odin—but some finds its way to human beings, giving them the godly power of imagination or poetry.

The *Ynglingasaga* tells another story of the truce between Vanir and Aesir. As was the Norse custom, the Vanir sent two hostages to the Aesir as a guarantee of peace. These were the gods Njord and Freyr. The Aesir sent the handsome Hoenir and the wise Mimir to the Vanir. Feeling that they had the worst of the exchange, the Vanir cut off Mimir's head and returned it to the Aesir, but Odin used his magic spells to make the head talk and to reveal many important secrets. Decapitation and talking heads figure also in Celtic mythology, as, for instance, in the case of the Welsh Bran, whose head went on talking long after his death.

Odin and the Other Gods

Clearly, the high god of the Germanic world was Odin (Wodan, Wotan, Woden). Odin is the "Allfather," but not a loving one. From his place in the gods' home, Asgard, where he lives with his wife, Frigg, he can see all there is to see in all the worlds of the universe. In his Zeus-like willingness to stir up trouble among those below him, he is closer to the trickster Loki than to his much-respected son Thor. In fact, shamanic qualities that associate him with the dead and with a magical knowledge of runes make him a trickster himself or at least a version of the magician-king. The mysterious self-sacrifice described in the *Havamal* depicts the shaman-trickster hanging on the world axis tree Yggdrasill—literally Ygg's or Odin's horse—a kenning, as Jaan Puhvel points out, for the gallows (194):

> I know I hung
> on the windswept tree,
> through nine days and nights.
> I was stuck with a spear
> and given to Odin,
> myself given to myself ...

In this hanging, Odin initiates rites of hanging and stabbing that were associated with his cult. The etymology of his name suggests divine inspiration, and he hangs on the tree to learn the runic mysteries guarded by Mimir's head at the end of one of Yggdrasill's roots. The *Voluspa* in the *Poetic Edda* tells how Odin sacrificed one of his eyes in return for a drink of the magical liquid of Mimir's well. Like the gigantic Balor in Irish mythology— Odin was descended from giants—his single eye had paralyzing power.

Odin is perhaps above all a terrifying god of battle, and he is god of the dead, a northern Dis Pater. He entertains brave fallen warriors at Valhalla (Vaholl, hall of the slain), and he inspires followers known as the *berserkir*—those who go berserk in battle, in the manner of other Indo-European warriors such as the Indian Karna, the Greek Achilles, and the Irish Cuchulainn.

The god Tyr, so important as the German Tiwaz (Tiw), part of the Wodan-Tiwaz-Thunr tripartite arrangement, plays a relatively minor role in the north. He is a war god who also protects judicial assemblies and is concerned with oaths, particularly those associated with the Germanic tradition of trial by ordeal. One of the few existing myths of Tyr tells of a strange trial by ordeal in which the trickster Loki, the vicious wolf Fenrir, and Tyr play major roles. In this myth, Tyr, like the Irish Nuada in his battle with the Firbolg, sacrifices a hand.

The Binding of Fenrir

Loki—although married to Sigyn—fathered three monstrous offspring by the giantess Angrboda. These were Fenrir the wolf, Jormungand the serpent, and Loki's ghastly daughter Hel; this last one— although human in form—stood out in a crowd as much as her brothers did. A normal and healthy woman from the waist up, from her waist down her flesh was rotten and blackened, and her expression was ever grim. The gods, warned of trouble by prophecy, hastened to cast Jormungand and Hel out of Asgard. Thus the serpent was thrust into the ocean around Midgard, where it grew and grew until it encircled the world, taking its own tail in its mouth. Likewise was Hel exiled to Niflheim, where she was granted sway over those who died of sickness and age. Fenrir, however, was allowed to remain in Asgard, the better to keep an eye on him.

He grew larger and more fierce by the day, and Tyr alone of all the gods was brave enough to feed him huge hunks of meat, which Fenrir swallowed whole, bones and all. Finally, the gods decided that they must rid themselves of the menace in their midst, but they were loathe to despoil the sanctuary of Asgard with blood spilled in anger. The course of action they resolved upon, therefore, was to bind the wolf. The gods attempted to hide their purpose in the guise of a contest, and appealing to Fenrir's vanity they challenged him to break the strongest bonds they could devise. The first two times the gods bound Fenrir in great fetters, the second more massive than the first, but both times the wolf burst his bonds with ease. Driven to the point of desperation, the gods bargained with the dwarfs to devise a bond strong enough to hold Fenrir. After some time the dwarfs produced a slim and silky cord that they made of six substances: the noise of a moving cat, the beard of a woman, the root of a mountain, the sinew of a bear, the breath of a fish, and the spit of a bird. Although the gods couldn't help but doubt that this thin ribbon would succeed where mighty chains had failed, they invited Fenrir to sail out to an island in a lake, where they approached him a third time with their challenge.

Suspicious of this turn of events, Fenrir at first refused to be bound by the cord; he was persuaded only when Tyr agreed to place his arm in Fenrir's mouth as a surety of the good faith of the gods. As soon as the cord was tied around him Fenrir began to struggle, but this time his bonds only tightened with every movement. As his predicament became clear to him, Fenrir bit down upon Tyr's arm, severing it at the elbow. Now the gods tied the cord to a mighty chain, which in turn they looped through a large stone; this stone they drove well into the earth, topping it with another boulder. Finally, the gods drove a sword through Fenrir's two jaws, gagging him.

Thus the three bastards of Loki and Angrboda were cursed and im-

prisoned by the gods, powerless to free themselves until the day of Ragnarok, when they would join their father in the overthrow of their keepers. The price for the imprisonment of Fenrir was the loss of the strong arm of Tyr, as well as the smirching of his honor (Fee and Leeming, 25–6).

Easily the most popular of the Norse gods was Thor, the northern version of the German Thunr. Thor is the god of sky and thunder, preserver of law and order in Midgard. As the son of the sky god Odin and the earth goddess Fyorgyn (Earth), he is also a god of fertility. Thor is dependable where Odin is unpredictable. Above all, he is steadfast in the struggle of the gods against the Giants. He retains the Herculean characteristics that the Romans had recognized in Thunr. Huge in size, with red beard and eyes, he has enormous appetites and not much wit. He carries a great hammer and wears iron gloves and a girdle of power. Thor's wife is the fertility goddess Sif, whose beautiful wheatlike hair was once shaved off—that is, stolen—by Loki. His daughter is Thrud, whose name, appropriately, means might.

Of particular significance is Thor's hammer, Mjollnir. Flung through the sky, it is a deadly weapon and is, of course, representative of lightning and thunder. Hammers representing Thor's fertile phallic power were traditionally placed in the laps of brides in Scandinavia. Such hammers were also used to hallow the newly born, perhaps to ensure fertile lives. Stories of Thor are among the most popular in Germanic mythology. In the myth that follows, Thor is the Indo-European giant-monster killer, the representative of good against evil, light against darkness.

Thor's Duel with Hrungnir

One fine day when Thor was off hunting trolls and their unsavory kin, Odin despaired of the amusements in Valhalla and thought to seek adventure abroad in Jotunheim. Donning one of his host of disguises, the Allfather leapt upon the back of Sleipnir and galloped off to the home

of Hrungnir, the greatest, stoniest, and most dangerous of all the giants. Hrungnir saw Odin riding toward him for some way across the
plains, and his curiosity, such as it was, was piqued. The giant com-
plimented his mysterious visitor on the lines and speed of his mount,
but received only boasts and taunts in return. When the stranger's insults turned to the subject of Hrungnir's own horse, Gold Mane, the
giant could bear them no more and hurried into the saddle himself to
take off after his visitor, capture him, and teach him a lesson. Odin's
taunts were not without merit, however, for although Gold Mane was
swift, Sleipnir was the swifter. Before he knew it, the giant found himself no longer in pursuit, but rather the cornered quarry himself: he had
followed Odin right through the gates of Asgard.

Hrungnir grew anxious for himself when he realized his predicament, but it was his luck that Thor was off elsewhere that day, and
Odin offered his giant adversary the sanctuary of hospitality. Soon
Hrungnir was drinking from Thor's own horn, filling the vast Hall of
the Slain with hot air as he repaid his hosts with nothing but taunting
words: boasts of his own prowess, threats and curses for the gods and
the fallen heroes surrounding him, and promises of amorous attention
to the beautiful goddesses Sif and Freya. The company quickly tired
of the lout's drunken ramblings, and Odin quietly sent for Thor. The
thunderer soon appeared, and his rage was the mightier when he
noted the drunken giant ogling Sif while Freya herself waited upon the
churlish oaf. When Thor reached for his hammer, however, Hrungnir
sobered up enough to remind the god of his own sacred status as a
guest, and an unarmed one at that. Thor relented when his honor
was questioned, and he quickly assented to Hrungnir's invitation to
single combat; no foe had ever dared issue such a challenge to the
thunder god before. A date was set and a place—the House of the
Stone Fence, on the border between Jotunheim and Asgard—and the
drunken giant made his exit.

The other giants thought that Hrungnir had won great honor through
his challenge of Thor, but they also feared what might happen to them
all if their champion should fall. To hedge their bets, then, they deter-

mined to create a massive giant out of clay; this creature was the biggest giant by far—taller even than Hrungnir himself—but he was made only of clay, not of stone, and he had for a heart only that of a slaughtered mare. They named their creation Mist Calf, and they commanded him to await Thor at the appointed place. On the chosen day the thunderer mounted his chariot with Thialfi by his side, and his passage was tempestuous: lightning flashed, thunder crashed, sparks flew from the wheels of Thor's cart, and the very earth itself seemed to roil and buckle with the god's anger. Mist Calf's terror was such that— as the god approached—a cascade of urine flooded from the trembling clay giant; Thialfi's ax made short work of Hrungnir's second.

Hrungnir himself was more steadfast and determined, however, and he cast his mighty whetstone at Thor just as the storm god sent Mjollnir end-over-end toward his foe; the two weapons intersected with a mighty cataclysm, and the whetstone was pulverized into a thousand fragments. Those pieces that landed in Midgard are the sources for whetstones even today. A large chunk of stone also found its way to Thor, who was knocked off of his feet by the force of the impact; stunned and bleeding profusely, Thor soon discovered that he had a great piece of lodestone imbedded in his head. His wound and mighty headache were not the end of Thor's problems, however; although his hammer had found its mark and ended Hrungnir's boasts and insults forever, the giant had fallen over the body of the god, and Thor found that he couldn't budge. Thialfi could not help either, and so he brought the gods, who all likewise failed in the task of shifting Hrungnir's corpse. Finally Thor's bastard Magni—his son by the giantess Jarnsaxi—was allowed to try, and he lifted the giant off of his father with ease. For this Thor gave Gold Mane to Magni, although Odin chafed at this gift as he had coveted the horse for himself.

Once home, Thor sent for Groa, the wife of Aurvandil, a woman of uncommon powers and mystical gifts. Groa worked her magic on Thor's wound, saying spells over him and using charms to work the stone out of his skull. Toward daybreak the sorceress had almost completed her magic, the stone was nearly out, and the pain had all but

*completely faded away. To show Groa his gratitude for her services,
Thor took her out to view the dawn sky, telling her that her husband—whom she had long presumed lost—would soon rejoin her.
Thor knew this to be the case because he himself had helped Groa's
husband to escape from Jotunheim, nearly frozen but quite alive. As
proof, the god pointed to a new star he had formed from Aurvandil's
frost-bitten big toe. No good deed goes unpunished, however; Groa's
joy at this news was such that her spells went out of her head and her
arts failed her. Thus, Thor in his first single combat had his victory
over Hrungnir and the giants lost their greatest champion; but the
whetstone remained forever lodged in the thunderer's head* (Fee and
Leeming, 38–9).

The most important of the Norse fertility gods—the Vanir—
belong to the family of Njord. Freyr and his sister Freya (Freyja)
are the children of Njord (Njordr) and his sister. The Vanir, as
fertility deities, recognize few sexual taboos. Njord's later marriage is to the giantess Skadi. The betrothal of Skadi and Njord
is told in this bawdy story involving the trickster Loki.

The Marriage of Njord and Skadi

*Skadi was a creature of the mountains and the scree, of the tundra
and the vast wastes: she was a huntress beyond compare, and she
brought death and destruction, gliding silently across the snows.
Skadi was the daughter of Thiazi the Giant, who with the aid of the
ever-duplicitous and self-serving Loki kidnapped Idun, the keeper of
the apples of youth precious to the gods: it was Thiazi's hope to defeat
the gods through their own age and decline. His plan went awry,
however, and the gods finished him instead. His daughter waited for
him at home in vain, and soon enough it became apparent to her that
the gods had gotten the best of her father.*

*Arming herself with the choicest of her father's arms and armor,
Skadi plotted vengeance. Smoldering with rage, the snowshoe goddess
made her way to Asgard.*

Having regained their eternal youth and savoring the bounty of life as never before, the gods were anxious to avoid further conflict and death. Thus, when Skadi came upon them in anger, the Aesir made haste to sue for peace. Skadi had already inherited her father's vast wealth and so was in no mood to take gold for his blood. She did, however, lack a husband, and she no longer took joy in life now that her father was gone. Therefore she stated these terms to the gods: the price for peace was to be marriage and mirth. She wished to pick a husband from among her foes, and she demanded that one among them make her laugh as she had never laughed before in her life. These terms seeming both just and easily accomplished, the gods agreed. The wily Odin put one condition upon this pact, however: Skadi was to choose her mate by the beauty of his feet and his feet alone.

Skadi quickly assented to Odin's condition, reasoning that Baldr, the most beautiful of the gods, surely walked upon the comeliest feet. The gods were then arranged before the giantess, but with a screen concealing them from their ankles up. It took but a little while to determine her choice, for to Skadi one pair of feet was clearly superior to all the rest: these she took to be Baldr's, and she chose him who possessed them. Skadi was soon disillusioned, however, as when the screen was lowered, she found herself looking into the eyes of Njord, lord of the sea and its fruits. Skadi complained that she had been duped, but it was too late, for the vow had been sworn and her choice made. Still, Skadi had not yet laughed, and she quickly reminded the gods that their arrangement would be null and void if she didn't receive her full measure of mirth.

At this point Odin called over Loki, knowing well that if anyone could accomplish this feat, it would be the trickster. At first Loki proclaimed his ineptitude; he said that he could not make Skadi laugh until he had related the tale of his morning's adventure with a billy goat. Loki then produced a thong, which he proceeded to tie to the beard of the goat. The god had been leading the goat to market in this way, he explained, but as his hands were full of other goods, he had

had to make use of his scrotum to anchor the tether: this part of his tale told, he proceeded to tie himself to the goat in this manner by way of illustration. Loki then made a loud noise, mimicking the sound that he claimed had startled the goat on the way to market. At this clamor the goat leapt forward, and the god and the goat began a protracted and farcical tug of war. Finally, with a last sharp thrust of Loki's hips, the goat lost its purchase on the turf and flew back into the trickster, knocking him over and into Skadi's arms. At this sight the giantess laughed long and loud, and for a moment she forgave Loki and the gods for her grief.

Leaving Asgard together, Skadi and Njord each wished to live in the way to which each had grown accustomed; therefore they agreed to divide their time between their domains. For nine nights they would sleep in Skadi's fastness of Thrymheim in the icy north, with the cry of the arctic wolf for a lullaby; the next nine nights they would pass in Njord's harbor home of Noatun, where the gulls and swans would lull them to sleep. Thus they lived together for some time, each at home in turn; but their life styles and tastes proved too different, and they soon had to live apart. Njord could not stand the silence or the barrenness of the icy mountains and flat tundra, and Skadi for her part detested the bustle, activity, and constant noise of the busy port. Though they remained married, then, they went their separate ways. and the frigid wastes of Skadi's heart—which had warmed a bit with the love of the god of the fertile sea—froze solid once more. Thus the love of the giantess was like the brief but spectacular growing season of her homeland, which thaws with the midnight sun of high summer, but freezes again quickly with the early onset of autumn, and is all but dead in the darkest months of winter (Fee and Leeming, 45–6).

Njord's children, Freyr and Freya, are even more obviously depicted as fertility deities, forming a triad with their father. Freyr and his father are perhaps related etymologically to the old Germanic goddess Nerthus, whom Tacitus called the Earth Mother.

In the more militantly patriarchal world of the north, Nerthus is masculinized. Freyr, the great god who regulates the sun, the rain, the produce of the land, and human fertility, is depicted, logically, with a gigantic phallus. The feminine aspect of the fertility triad, Freya, is a goddess of both war and love, and is known for her lascivious ways, even giving sexual favors to four dwarfs in return for her primary symbol of fertility, the necklace of the Brisings.

The highest ranking of the goddesses is Frigg, the wife of Odin. Born of Fjorgyn, the earth goddess. Frigg shares her husband's knowledge of human destiny. She is the grieving mother of the dying god Baldr, and she is associated with childbirth. In the obvious fertility connection between Freya and Frigg (Freya's husband is Od, whose name, therefore, relates him to Odin, and Odin often desires Freya), Kevin Crossley-Holland suggests a possible remnant of the old Indo-European triune goddess (like Hera, Aphrodite, and Artemis, for example), with Skadi representing the huntress aspect (p. xxx).

Central to many of the Norse myths is Loki, the shape-shifting trickster offspring of the Giants, who is at once charming, mischievous, and evil. Nowhere is Loki's role more important than in the myth of the beautiful god Baldr, son of Odin and Frigg.

Loki and the Death of Baldr

When Baldr the Beautiful, son of the high god Odin, had dreams foreshadowing his destruction, the gods intervened to save him. His mother, Frigg, convinced everything on earth to swear not to harm her son. Only one small plant, the mistletoe, was overlooked. Believing Baldr was now immune to any threat, the gods enjoyed throwing things at him for fun. But the trickster Loki, in female disguise, learned from Frigg of the neglected mistletoe. He plucked it out of the earth and convinced the blind god Hod (Hodr) to throw the plant at his brother Baldr. Loki guided the god's hand, and the mistletoe struck its victim in the heart, causing instant death.

The gods were bitterly sad at the loss of so wonderful a companion, and Odin realized that Baldr's death foreshadowed the death of all the gods. Frigg called on a volunteer to travel to Hel to bring her son back. Another of her sons, Hermod, agreed to go. He rode to Hel, found Baldr seated in a place of honor, and learned that the god could return to earth only if all things, living and dead, would weep for him. When Odin learned the news of his son, he called on all things to weep. And all things did weep—all but a giantess, the disguised Loki in fact, who snarled, "Let Hel keep her own." And so Baldr was to remain in the land of the dead until the world would revive after its destruction (Fee and Leeming, 84–5).

With the death of Baldr, Ragnarok, the end of the world, is inevitable.

Ragnarok

At last the doom of the gods will fall upon them; Gullinkambi, the golden cock of Asgard, will waken Odin's hosts. His cousins in Hel and Jotunheim will crow likewise. The strife of man against man and brother against brother will increase and not abate. The Great Winter will fall, three years long, and the snows will bury life, the winds will quench it, and the sun will give no respite. The wolf Skoll will swallow the sun, and Hati will devour the moon; their gore will splatter earth and heavens. The stars will flicker and die. The earth will shake and quake, and all Yggdrasill will tremble. The old bonds will be no more. Loki the trickster and Fenrir the wolf will burst free, and the seas will overlap their shores with a violent tide as Jormungand— the great Midgard serpent—makes his way to shore. Naglfar—the ghastly ship made of the nails of dead men—will sail to battle. Loki will captain the ship of the dead from Hel, and Hrim will command a bursting load of giants. Fenrir's wide jaws will scrape both heaven and earth, and Jormungand will spew venom and poison throughout creation. Surt will lead the fire demons of Muspell across Bifrost, the Rainbow Bridge, and it will shatter and fall beneath them; fire will encompass them, and Surt's sword will take the place of the sun. The enemies of the gods will gather on the plain of Vigrid, and they will be terrible to behold.

The gods will be no less prepared. Heimdalr will call a blast on his mighty Gjallarhorn, and the gods will rush to assemble. Odin will leap upon Sleipnir and hasten to consult Mimir, while the Aesir and the Einherjar arm themselves; they will don helm and mailcoat, and grasp sword, shield, and spear. Eight hundred strong will march shoulder-to-shoulder through each of Valhalla's five hundred and forty doors; they will be led to Vigrid by Odin, resplendent in golden helm and shining mail. He will grip Gungnir grimly. Odin will greet Fenrir with cold cheer, and Thor beside him will look to settle his old score with Jormungand. The serpent will prove a match for the thunderer; Odin may expect to have no help from that quarter. Freyr will grapple with Surt, and well might he rue the day he pledged his mighty blade to Skirnir. After a great struggle. Freyr falls to the fiery sword of Surt. Tyr and Garm the Hound each will prove the death of the other, and Loki and Heimdalr likewise will even ancient enmity. Thor will best Jormungand in the end, but will live to step back only nine paces before he succumbs to the poison the serpent spewed upon him. Fenrir will swallow the one-eyed god at the last, but his victory will be cut short by Vidar, who will avenge his father and vanquish the wolf by stepping on its lower jaw and stretching the other up until he rips it asunder. Vidar's shoe that day will take all of time to cobble; it will be made of all of the scraps of leather ever snipped off of shoe leather and cast away, and it will prove too thick and tough even for the fangs of Fenrir. Then Surt will cast his fire through the three levels and nine worlds of creation, and all will die: men and gods, dwarfs and elves, birds and beasts, all manner of creatures and monsters. The sun will be extinguished, the stars drowned. and the earth will sink beneath the waves (Fee and Leeming, 144).

But out of Ragnarok, as out of the endings of the ancient Indian eras, a new world will be born.

The Return of Baldr

The earth will rise from the deeps again one day, green and blossoming, and crops will flourish where none were planted. A new sun will take the place of her mother, and a number of gods will return to the ancient ruins of Asgard, led now by Baldr. Lif and Lifthrasir will survive to renew the race of men; they will have hidden themselves securely in Yggdrasill's embrace. And the fire of Surt will not scorch them; they will survive on the morning dew, and keep watch through the branches above them for the new sun rising. And thus, through its death, the world will be born again.

Certain similarities exist between the myths of King Arthur and those of the Norse Baldr, suggesting a possible single source for both stories. As Arthur was slain by his son or nephew, Baldr was killed by his brother, and as the wounded Arthur was cared for by women, Baldr was sometimes associated with the supernatural warrior-women called the Valkyries. Like Arthur, he partook of magical food. Furthermore, his death, like Arthur's with its promise of return, can be tied to the idea of fertility.

Scholars have long sought Baldr's origins in the fertility gods of the Middle East, gods such as Attis, Baal, Adonis, and Osiris, who died and returned with the plants of spring. Baldr's particular plant, the mistletoe—the one Snorri tells us killed him—attaches itself to the oak, a sacred tree not only to the Celts but to Indo-Europeans in general (Fee and Leeming, 144, 136).

Later northern Christians would see in Baldr a prophecy of the new Christian god who, after *his* return from the dead, as we learn from the Anglo-Saxon *Dream of the Rood*, "surrounded by the mighty host of souls He had freed from the torments of Hell—returned to the City of God crowned with victory and glory" (Fee and Leeming, 87).

7

Baltic, Slavic, and Balkan Mythology

The Balts and Their Mythology

Baltic peoples included Latvians, Lithuanians—not Christianized until the early fifteenth century—and Old Prussians, who inhabited what is now eastern Germany and the Baltics and land extending as far east as Moscow beginning in about the middle of the second millennium B.C.E. By the first millennium the Balts, whose languages are closer to the ancient Indo-European Vedic language than any other European language group, had developed from a hunter-gatherer culture into an agricultural one. Not surprisingly, then, what little we know of Baltic mythology is a combination of perhaps very ancient nature deities and deities closely associated with farming and fertility.

Baltic mythology has not received the scholarly attention devoted to other Indo-European mythologies, partly because of the continuous subjugation of Balts by their neighbors over the centuries and the consequent contamination of the old religion by Christianity and other mythologies, particularly Germanic and Slavic. In recent years, however, more concentrated scholarly work has been done by Marija Gimbutas, Haralds Biezais, Jaan Puhvel, and others.

The Baltic Pantheons

It is mainly through folklore, contained primarily in folk songs (Latvian *dainas*, Lithuanian *dainos*) typically sung at significant rites of passage, and Russian and German chronicles of the tenth through seventeenth centuries that we discover the remnants of the old Baltic religion and its pantheon. In about 1520 Simon Grunau in his *Prussian Chronicle* revealed something of the Old Prussian aspect of Baltic mythology, at the center of which was a typically Indo-European triad. The triad—somewhat resembling the king-priest god, warrior god-thunder god, fertility-god triad represented by the Norse Odin-Thor-Freyr—was made up of Patollo (Pecullus, Pikoulis), Perkuno, and Potrimpo. All were associated with a sacred oak tree. Of these deities, Patollo was apparently the most important. He was depicted as an old man with a great green beard and was associated with the skulls of humans and, in keeping with the most ancient of Indo-European traditions, cows and horses. Patollo was, like Dis Pater, a god of the dead. Later, in his more folkloric Christianized status as Pecullus, he became the devil. A possible Lithuanian version of this high god is Velinus, like Odin, a terrifying one-eyed deity associated with hanging. He is also, like the Greek Hades, a kidnapper of maidens, but he sometimes favors the poor and downtrodden. For Baltic Christians, Velinus was also sometimes associated with the devil.

The second aspect of the original triad, Perkuno—Perkunas in Lithuania, Piorun in Poland, and Perkons in Latvia—was depicted as a fully mature god with a black beard and eyes of fire. He is essentially synonymous with the Slavic Perun. A perpetual fire was apparently kept alive in connection with his worship. As his name indicates, Perkuno (thunder) was the thunder god who, like his Norse relative Thor, seems to have been more popular than the nominal head god, and his cult survived the coming of Christianity, especially in times of drought when farmers would sacrifice animals to the god as a source of fertility, drink beer in his honor, and dance around a bonfire in hopes of stimulating rain.

Perkuno, as the god of cleansing rain, was also the god of justice and moral order. So it was that he killed Jurate, goddess of the sea, because of her sexual involvement with a mortal, and broke the face of the moon god Menuo into what became the phases of the moon as a punishment for that god's desire for and in some stories kidnapping of Ausrine (dawn or the planet Venus, also known as Auseklis), the daughter of Saule, the sun goddess. There is one story that suggests that the attack on Menuo (Meness) is in support of the thunder god's own affair with Ausrine. Perkuno in some places is seen as a smith god who molds the world into existence.

The third god in the triad, Potrimpo, is depicted as a happy beardless youth with ears of grain. Clearly he is a Pan-like god of fertility. The triad had its earthly brahman-type priests— equivalents of the Celtic druids, or the Roman *flamines*—called by Grunau in German *waidolotten*.

Haralds Biezais outlines a Baltic pantheon that is presided over by a sky-god creator who in all likelihood preceded the rise of Perkuno to divine dominance in the Baltics and remained important especially in Lithuania. This god's name, Dievs in Latvia, Dievas in Lithuania and Old Prussia, is clearly related, like that of the Greek Zeus, to the Vedic Dyaus (from the Indo-European root dyeu meaning heavens). Dievs seems to have developed from a representation of the sky to a personification of the sky and then to a personal god (2:50). In his folkloric depiction, Dievs is a well-dressed farmer, complete with overcoat and mittens, who presides over a farm on a mountain in the heavens. In the good Indo-European tradition, he is associated with horses that pull his chariot around his farm. Sometimes he is equated with a solar god named Usins whose chariot, in Latvia, was said to be pulled by two white horses across the sky. Sometimes Usins was seen as one of a set of divine twins or sons of Dievs, known as the *Asvinai* or *Dievas Deli*, typical Indo-European horse gods, like the Vedic twins, the Aśvins, and the Greek Dioscuri (sons of god).

Dievs's sacred drink is beer, the mead of Baltic rituals, which has equivalents in other Indo-European cultures. In folklore Dievs is a highly personal and domestic god who at particular times in the Baltic mythological calendar visits with and advises earthly farmers. In this domestic aspect, he is unlike most Indo-European supreme deities and perhaps reminiscent of an older pre-Indo-European earth-centered religion. In one planting myth, Dievs spends the night with a group of farmers watching over the fire and the horses and by mistake leaves his mittens behind when he departs at sunrise.

The second god described by Biezais is the goddess Saule, whose name points to her solar nature. Saule, or Saules Mate (Mother Sun), like Dievs, must have begun as the natural phenomenon itself, become a personification, and eventually achieved a personal nature. According to some, Saules is constantly pursued by a would-be lover, the moon god Menuo. In other stories she is the wife of Dievs.

In places where they are not husband and wife, conflicts between Dievs and Saule arise because of things done by personifications of the stars, the Asvani, to the Saules Meitas (Daughters of the Sun). These actions are mirrored not only in the Baltic tradition of the ritual abduction of brides but in the theft of the brides Phoebe and Hilaeeria by the Greek Dioscuri. The conflicts between Saule and Dievs are not terribly important, however. Saule is a farming mother protecting her children, and in places where she is particularly honored she gives the world the gift of her warmth, riding, like Apollo, across the sky in her sun chariot. Saule is associated with the world oak tree, the *saules koks* (sun tree), the source of all fertility, that grows out of the heavenly mountain and has been seen by no mortal. This suggests that Saule is a relative of those pre-Indo-European great mothers of the world without whom there is no life. In Latvian folklore she walks across fields with her skirts raised as if to bring the fertility of her loins to the land.

Another version of the fertility goddess is Zeme (Zemyna in Lithuanian). She was originally earth itself and then a personification and personal goddess with 70 sisters who represent various aspects of nature—fields, mushrooms, elks, and so forth. Still other fertility deities are Ceroklis and Jumis. These and the Baltic gods in general have survived in the modern Baltic states in folkloric tradition even though they were officially replaced by the Christian god, whose fertility is spiritual, and later by political systems that for many years rejected both mythologies.

The Slavs and Their Mythology

Indo-European people known collectively as Slavs, speaking proto-Slavic, were active in central and eastern Europe at least as early as 800 B.C.E. By the tenth century C.E. a long process of separation had produced a western group speaking Polish, Czech, Slovak, and Wendish, an eastern group speaking Russian, Byelorussian, and Ukranian, and a southern group speaking Slovenian, Serbo-Croatian, Macedonian, and Bulgarian.

The fact that literacy, as in the case of other early European cultures, came to the Slavs only with Christianity in the ninth and tenth centuries means that relatively little is known of Slavic mythology. What we do know is derived primarily from folklore. There is also useful material in the writing of Christianized Slavs looking back at their pagan heritage. We learn something, for example, from the biographers of Otto, a twelfth-century bishop who struggled against remnants of the old religion in the north. The Byzantine historian Procopius is an important source, as is the Russian *Primary Chronicle*, dating from the early twelfth century and describing the pantheon established in Kiev in 980 by

Vladimir I of Russia before his subsequent Christianization in 988.

Slavic Pantheons

A major Slavic god whose four heads apparently represented the four directions and the four seasons was Svantovit (Sventovit, Swiantowid), who may be a western version of the eastern Slavic high god Swarog. In some places two of the god's heads are male, two female. Svantovit is at once a god of war and of fertility. Like many Slavic gods, he has direct Iranian antecedents as indicated by the root *svent* that connects with both the ideas of strength and of holiness in Iranian.

Other many-headed Slavic gods were the seven-faced Rujevit (Rugievit, Ruevit, Rinvit), perhaps an aspect of Svantovit representing autumn and facing east; the five-headed Porevit (Turupit, Tarapita), representing summer and south; the war god Iarovit (Jarovit, Dzarowit, Gerovit, Gerovitus, and perhaps Jarilo), who represents spring and faces west, the four-faced Porenutius (Potenut, Puruvit), and the three-headed Triglav, whose triune aspect apparently marked his watching over the three major realms—sky, earth, and underworld. Gods with more than one head are, as we have seen, clearly within the Indo-European tradition.

Also present among the Slavs was Tjarnaglofi or Veles (Weles, Volos), the black god or horned god, a version of the Indo-European underworld or dark god, who may have evolved into the Slavic Christian Satan. His opposite was the sun god, the god of light, who takes many forms in various Slavic areas (Svantovit himself or Dazhbog-Khors). In some traditions Dazhbog-Khors is a son of Svantovit.

Marija Gimbutas points out that solar god myths are common in Slavic folklore, and she tells the story of the personified sun driving his golden chariot across the sky, changing from youth to old man as he goes. With him go two virgins, personifications of the morning and evening stars, and seven judges representing the seven planets ("Slavic Religion," 13:356). The solar god has a bald relative who is the moon.

Gimbutas also suggests the similarity between the Slavic opposition between gods of darkness and light and that between the Baltic Dievas and Velinus. As noted above, she suggests that several of the Slavic gods represent, like their counterparts in the Baltic tradition, the aging process of the year ("Slavic Religion," 13:356). An important Hephaistos-like smith-solar-fire god is Swarog (Svarogu among eastern Slavs, but perhaps the same as Svantovit). Swarog is father of the sun (Dazhbog-Khors) and is highly sexual. He is sometimes identified with Swarozhicz, personified fire, whose name, however means Son of Swarog. Bialobog (similar to Czarnobog, his brother) is another black god representing winter and north. He is a bent old man with beard and staff, resembling the common image of Father Time or Saturn. Most of these names and the light-dark duality suggest Iranian influence.

Perun (Proven) the thunder god, who is clearly related to the Baltic Perkuno (Perkunas), seems to have been for many Slavs the most important god, as Thor was to many Germanic peoples and Perkuno was to many Balts. His name is etymologically associated with the oak tree, sacred to so many Indo-European gods. His animals are the bull and the goat, representing power and fertility. He carries an ax and arrows symbolizing thunder and lightning. In the Russian tradition, Perun, like the Indian gods Siva and Indra, is a monster-slayer who releases the waters of fertility. Sacrifices were made to Perun, and a sacramental, communal meal following the sacrifice would blend well into the later arrival of the Christian tradition of Holy Communion.

A Slavic god of particular importance to the eventual emergence of Christianity was Jarilo (Iarilo), a Dionysos-like god of youth and spring, wearing a crown of flowers. This was the Slavic version of Adonis-Dionysos-Balder, the dying and resurrected god of fertility.

Another Slavic deity with European counterparts is Lada, the goddess of love, who differs from Aphrodite, however, in that she, like Jarilo, is a dying and rising deity. She is sometimes seen as one of a pair of divine twins, sometimes as the wife of the great god Swarog as a cocreator of the world. A goddess named Dziewona is the counterpart huntress to Artemis-Diana.

In the pantheon of Vladimir I, Perun is the supreme god. With him are Khursu (Khors), Dazibogu (Dahzbog), Stribogu (Stribog), Simariglu, and a single goddess, Mokosi (Mokosh, Mokysha, Mokusha), whose name refers to wetness and is at least in part derived from the Iranian tradition. The moist goddess is sometimes Corn Mother, the spirit of grain. She is in all likelihood the same as Matka or Mata Syra Zjemlja around whom Dionysian-like Slavic earth rituals were performed well into Christian times. As was the case with so many European goddesses of the earth, Mokosi was later assimilated into the person of the Virgin Mary, perhaps especially in her earth-colored form as the Black Madonna so popular in Poland and in other parts of Europe.

Another popular goddess to emerge from folklore, is Baba Yaga, whom Gimbutas ties to the Old European goddess of death ("Slavic Religion," 13:359). Baba Yaga can appear to be young or old and has the ancient great-goddess association with birds and snakes. She is sometimes depicted as a flying witch whose vehicle was a mortar with a pestle used as a rudder. Her turning house rested on chicken legs and was surrounded by a fence made of human bones. The keyhole of the front door contained teeth. Clearly Baba Yaga is a Slavic version of Kālī, the terrifying Indian black goddess of annihilation.

Various mythic heroes emerge from the Slavic tradition, primarily from Russian epics. These include Volkh (Volga), a major shapeshifter with similarities to Odin and Sigurd, whose father was a dragon. Svjatogar is a Herculean strongman, and Mikula is a larger-than-life plowman who represents agriculture.

When Russia was officially Christianized in 988, Perun's statue was tied to a horse's tail and dragged through the streets before being thrown into the river. But the god remains a folkloric fertility figure for farmers today, as do Corn Mother and many other deities. And many of the Slavic deities have been assimilated by the Christian tradition. Perun himself became Saint Il'ia, who also crosses the sky in his chariot. Veles became the devil, as Velinus did in the Baltics.

Balkan Mythology

In the south—the present-day Balkans—Slavs encountered and at least partly assimilated Albanian-speaking Indo-Europeans whose linguistic and cultural ancestors are possibly the Illyrians, an ancient people mentioned by Homer as allies of the Trojans against the Greeks (Mallory, 73–76). Other Indo-European Balkan tribes were Thracians and their relatives the Geto-Dacians, a version of whose language still exists in Romania. Herodotus claimed that the Thracians were the second largest tribe on earth. They too are listed among the enemies of the Greeks at Troy. The Greeks believed that both Dionysos and Orpheus came from Thrace. In telling the story that would possibly become the source for Euripides' *The Bacchae*, Homer tells of the struggle between Dionysos—perhaps synonymous with Sabazios—and the Thracian king Lykurgos, who, as noted earlier, was probably the source for Pentheus in Euripides' work (*Iliad*, 5). Other Thracian divinities known to the Greeks included two goddesses whose origins are perhaps pre-Indo-European. These were the goddesses Bendis and Cotys. The Greeks associated both with their Artemis. Cotys, whose cult involved men dressing as women, would seem to be related, like the Thracian Dionysos, to the Euripidean story of the demise of the feminized Pentheus at the hands of the orgiastic maenads, who punish the king for denying their god. As for the Geto-Dacians, their mythology was dominated by Zalmoxis, a divine king whose Pythagorian philosophy promised immortality to his followers, making him, like Dionysos, a natural forerunner to the Christian man-god who would eventually come to dominate Europe. Gimbutas suggests an influence on the agricultural, goddess-centered aspect of Slavic mythology from both the Baltic peoples of the north and the Thracians and Geto-Dacians of the south ("Slavic Religion," 13:354).

8

Finnic and Other
Non-Indo-European Mythologies

Clearly, the dominant tradition in European mythology is that of the Indo-Europeans. There were, however, pockets of non-Indo-European mythology that survived into the historical period. We have already noted the importance of Minoan mythology for the Greeks and Etruscan mythology for the Romans, for instance. Other important mythologies existed in Spain.

Tartessians, Turdetans, Iberians, and Basques

When the Romans, Celts, and others made their way to Spain, they encountered Tartessians, non-Indo-Europeans who, influenced by Phoenician traders and like the Romans, had adopted the goddess Astarte and who celebrated Habis, a culture hero who was responsible for the establishment of Tartessian customs. Another non-Indo-European culture in Spain were the Turdetans, who also worshipped Astarte. Iberians in Spain developed a cult around the somewhat similar goddess Tanit, a figure with Greek-inspired Artemis-like qualities (see Blazquez, "Ibesian Religion," 6:547–51).

The language and culture of the non-Indo-European Basques,

who inhabit the mountainous region between Spain and France, have survived defiantly into the present era. Their mythology was greatly influenced by the mythologies of the Celts and the Romans but also developed patterns familiar to students of the Neolithic period. The existence of *lamniaks*, female figures with bird or fish characteristics, points back to the goddesses of ancient Europe. Another important Basque goddess is Mari, a rain deity associated like many ancient goddesses with a serpent husband. The Basque blacksmith-grain god Basajaun has been compared to the Roman Silvanus, a nature deity (Blazquez, "Basque Religion," 2:80).

The Finno-Ugrians

The most significant and widespread of the non-Indo-European mythologies of Europe, however, is that of the Finnic-Ugric-speaking peoples whose original Uralic language (spoken by peoples of the northern Urals from at least 6000 B.C.E.) divided in about 4000 B.C.E. into Finno-Ugric west of the Urals and Samoyed mostly, but not exclusively, to the east. There are those who argue from linguistic evidence that proto-Indo-European and proto-Uralic must have derived from a single proto-Indo-Uralic language (Mallory, 149). Be that as it may, by 3000 B.C.E. the Finno-Ugric peoples, driven by the processes of fishing, hunting, and gathering, had broken up into two primary subfamilies—Finnic and Ugric (or Ugrian)—and then into several smaller groups that would eventually develop somewhat distinct non-Indo-European mythologies and languages. The primary Ugric language and culture became what is now Hungarian. Of their mythology little is known other than the apparent dominance of shamanism, a belief in the afterlife, a high god, and a tradition of having descended from a female deer. One Hungarian origin myth tells how Queen Emesu had a dream in which she was fertilized by a goshawk, much as in Buddhist lore Queen

Māyā was fertilized in a dream by a white elephant. Queen Emesu's resulting offspring was Almus, the founder of a line of Hungarian chiefs who would lead the Hungarians to their present land.

The Finnic peoples became Permians (Permiaks and Udmurts in Russia), so-called Volga Finns (especially Mordvians and Mari or Cheremis, also in what is now Russia), and Baltic Finns (Karelians in Russia, Estonians in the Baltics, and Finns in what is now Finland). The Lapps (Saami) in northern Scandinavia and Russia are usually included, somewhat arbitrarily given their distinctness, in this latter group.

Many of the Volga and Permian peoples became agricultural and, not surprisingly, developed farmer-based myths that somewhat resemble those of the Balts discussed in chapter 7. The Udmurt Permians had a sky god called Inmar who was a farmer and a weather deity. Other farmer-sky gods existed among the Mordvians and the Mari. Also important for these farming peoples was the earth goddess, who in several areas was known as Corn Mother. Mordvians known as the Ezra and the Moksa worshiped Mastor-Ava, the earth mother responsible for the harvest. They also celebrated water goddesses.

The Lapps, who were hunters rather than farmers, were prone to totemic animal cults—especially that of the bear as animal lord, a tradition with roots in the Neolithic. Other animal spirits popular especially among the Lapps of Finland are the *haldi* who watched over aspects of nature. Some Lapps also had a thunder god called Tiermes, or in some places Horagalles, and other ruler-sky gods such as Radien or Vearalden, whose sacred sites were marked by a *stytto*, the symbol of a world tree or pillar that reached up to the North star. The Finns also had such a pillar. Several of the Lapp sky gods have been compared to the Samoyed sky god Num (Backman, 12:499).

The Baltic Finns especially were directly influenced by their Indo-European neighbors, the Germans, the Slavs, and the Balts.

A Finnish thunder-sky god called Ukko, with his hammer, club, and sword, resembles Thor and would later develop under Christianity into an image of the Christian god. The Finnish chief sky god was Jumala, whose name, like that of the Indo-European sky god, refers to the phenomenon of light.

Shamanism seems to have been an important influence on the mythology of most of the Finno-Ugric people. Thus, as sorcerer-shamans typically travel in various forms—including those of animals—between the worlds to negotiate with spirit powers, the Finno-Ugric creation myths usually involved the earth-diver pattern in which an animal is sent by a god to bring elements of earth from the depths of primal waters to create our world. Important in this connection was the concept of the great whirlpool that dragged unwary seagoing people down to the world of the water spirits. The land of the dead beneath the earth was also the home of spirits.

Many Finnish shamanic myths concern the Orpheus-like musician-enchanter Väinämöinen, often the creator-hero of an earth-diver, or more commonly a cosmic egg creation. In one famous story, Väinämöinen leads a group to a far land ruled by the Woman of the North to find the *sampo*, a mysterious and sacred instrument that could ensure prosperity and that in some stories was forged by the smith Ilmarinen.

Another central aspect of Finno-Ugric mythology is the emphasis on astronomy. The star formations, for example, were animal spirits. Several Milky Way myths exist in the Finno-Ugric system. In one, a giant oak tree—the *iso tammi* in Finland—that had been planted by three spirit girls had grown so large that it blocked the path of the clouds across the sky and obscured the sun and the moon. A tiny figure came out of the sea and proceeded to chop down the oak, making a path for the passing of the clouds and revealing the sun and moon. This same miniature being, or one much like him, was responsible for the constellation known as the *iso harka* (great ox).

The astronomical myths exist in the context of a complex Finno-Ugric cosmography in which the world is surrounded by a stream and covered by a canopy created in some versions by Ilmarinen and centered on the North Star-capped pillar mentioned above. In some stories the end of the world can occur with the collapse of the pillar. A world tree with celestial bodies in its branches exists along with a world mountain and a world navel at the center of the earth.

Kalevala

The most comprehensive collections of Finnic myths and legends is in the national epic of Finland, the *Kalevala*, a late (1835 and 1849) compilation of the poet Elias Lonnrot, based to a great extent on oral traditions from Karelia and elsewhere. Central characters in the epic are Väinämöinen, Ilmarinen, the rash hero Lemminkäinen, and Louhi, the mistress-ruler of North Farm.

The *Kalevala* begins with a creation myth in which a teal, searching for a nest, lands on the raised knee of the Mother of the Waters, a virgin who has descended from the sky to rest on the primal waters. The teal lays eggs that break when the virgin moves her knee, and the earth and celestial bodies are formed. The hero Väinämöinen is also born and the smith Ilmarinen creates the canopy of the heavens.

It is Väinämöinen who makes the wilderness fertile. After falling into the sea, he floats for a time until he is rescued and carried to North Farm, where Louhi is mistress. In return for a promise to allow the now-ancient Väinämöinen to marry her daughter, Louhi asks for the creation of the *sampo*, the great tripartite mill that can grind salt, grain, and gold, and Väinämöinen promises to send the crafstman Ilmarinen to make it.

Next comes the story of the death of the wild Lemminkäinen in the Land of the Dead and his resurrection through the magic of his mother.

Väinämöinen journeys back toward North Farm to ask for Louhi's daughter but discovers a rival in the form of the *sampo*-builder Ilmarinen. Ilmarinen is favored by the daughter but is forced to perform several Herculean labors if he wishes to marry her. As Medea helped Jason, the maiden helps her lover to accomplish the tasks.

Ilmarinen's wife is killed by wild animals substituted for her cattle by the war hero Kullervo, and in his despair, Ilmarinen tries to craft a new wife.

Eventually Ilmarinen, Väinämöinen, and Lemminkäinen, the heroes of Kalevala (Finland), put aside their differences and go off together to North Farm to capture the *sampo*. At first they succeed, but Louhi pursues them, and in a struggle at sea the *sampo* sinks. Väinämöinen retrieves bits and pieces of the *sampo* and Louhi manages to hold on to a piece of it. What follows is a long struggle between the Kalevala people and the forces of North Farm. In that struggle, Louhi sends plagues against Kalevala and hides the sun and moon, which eventually the heroes succeed in forcing her to release.

The poem ends with the departure of Väinämöinen, and the baptism of a new king of Karelia. The old world has given way to the new. A poet uses the abandoned sacred harp of Väinämöinen to accompany the final song of the epic.

PART 3

European Mythic Patterns
and Christian Hegemony

9

European Deities
and Creation Myths

THE CONCEPTS OF divinity and creation are pervasive in the human psyche. In Europe, as in every other section of the world, divinity has taken many forms. Indications of a great mother creatrix are evident, especially in the cave paintings of the European Paleolithic period and in the archeology of the Neolithic period. There are numerous examples of sovereign gods, warrior gods, thunder gods, fertility gods, and trickster gods. Images of godhead reflect people's sense of the nature of the universe, of life in general, and of particular cultural experience. For some, gods have been a literal presence; for others, gods have been metaphors for vague understandings of the mysteries of the universe and the psyche. Perhaps most importantly, humans have needed divinity to make sense of where we came from and of who and what we are. Both as a species and as cultures it is difficult to conceive of mere chance existence. We crave identity. As the one species blessed or cursed by the sense of plot—of beginnings, middles, and ends—we are driven to tell the essential story of where we came from and why. So we have gods who created us. And our images of creation say a great deal about who we are.

The deities and creation myths of Europe—Greek, Roman, Celtic, Germanic, Slavic, Baltic, Finnic, and others, as well as those Judeo-Christian concepts imported from the Middle East—are on the one hand elements of a European pattern, dominated, as we have seen, by a larger Indo-European pattern, and on the other hand projections of particular cultural experiences and social systems. The conflict between the goal of a single European entity and many cultural entities has been at the basis of European history from the Neolithic age to the present day. Europeans, like humans in other relatively restricted geographic areas, have struggled to achieve unity by force or persuasion, but they have been willing to die for their particular cultural identities and beliefs, beliefs embodied, for instance, in their gods and their various understandings of creation.

The chapters leading up to this section have been concerned with the particular cultural entities in Europe. The two chapters that follow will not abandon the recognition of these different cultures but will emphasize the larger European pattern through a collection of myths arranged by types, beginning with the major deities and creation and then turning to the myth of the hero.

Creation Myths

As cultures we identify ourselves through the collective dreams we call creation myths, or cosmogonies (from *kosmos* + *gonos* = universe + offspring). Creation myths explain in metaphorical terms our sense of who we are in the context of the world around us, and in so doing they reveal our real priorities, as well as our real prejudices. Cosmogonies are important for the same reason that our explorations of the personal past are important in psychoanalysis. Perhaps most of all, creation myths reveal our sense of our relationship with and the nature of our primal parents, our deities.

Earth Mother

The earliest myth-making inhabitants of the European continent, like early humans elsewhere, very likely thought of creation in terms of a feminine metaphor. The primary creative miracle in the purely animal and therefore human context was that of birth from the female. It would have made sense to transfer this experience to the primary miracle in the environment, the miracle of the birth and rebirth of plant life. The human need to explain the phenomenon and to express understandings in story and metaphor would have been the impetus for the emergence of the great goddess, the earth mother. Prehistoric evidence in Europe, as indicated in Chapter 1 and in the work of Marija Gimbutas and others, supports this hypothesis. The mother was still alive and well in the Minoan and Pelasgian mythologies discussed earlier, and remnants of her original power remained evident even in ancient cultures that were patriarchal, as, for instance, in the Greek Gaian creation myth that so resembles the earlier Pelasgian creation story.

The great goddess typically took a triune form. She was maiden, mother, and crone. She was the phases of nature—of the moon, of agriculture. She was birth, life, and death. In Greece she was Hebe the virgin cupbearer, Hera the wife and mother, and Hecate the crone of the moon and the underworld. Aspects of the triune goddess are found in Persephone (Kore) and her mother, Demeter, and the witness to Persephone's rape, Hecate. In some Orphic versions of the myth of Dionysos (Zeus-like or Zeus's son), Persephone is the god's mother. More often his mother is Semele, who is sometimes associated with the moon as Selene.

Among the pre-Roman Latin tribes, the goddess was worshipped as Uni—a single trinity made up of the maiden Juventas, the mother Juno, and the wise Minerva. Later, the Etruscans and early Romans, as we have seen, substituted the chief god Jupiter for Juventas, creating another kind of trinity altogether.

In the identification of the ancient gods of Celtic Ireland we find a clear remnant of ancient goddess power in the collective name of the gods as the Tuatha Dé Danaan, the sons of Danu, Danu being the ancient great goddess of the Celts. The Irish form of the great goddess has archetypal descendants. There are the eponymous queens—Eire, Banba, and Fotla—without whose presence there is no Ireland and no legitimate sovereignty. Another Irish expression of the triune female goddess is the warrior goddess Morrigan, the "great queen," who is also Macha, sometimes wife of the Tuatha king Nuada, sometimes queen of Ulster; Badb, who led battles with her terrifying war cry; and other war goddesses. She perhaps takes more human form in Queen Maeve (Medb), who plays an important role in the *Táin*.

Still other remnants of the old great goddess exist in figures such as the Germanic Freya; the Slavic Corn Mother; the Russian-Slavic Mokosh, the goddess of moisture, spinning, and fate; the Basque Mari; the Baltic sun goddess Saule; the Kālī-like Slavic Baba Yaga; and other goddesses whose powers even as fertility figures eventually become inferior to those of the great male gods when patriarchal warrior cultures dominate Europe. A particularly good example of such a goddess is Demeter, who retains her connection to and abode on earth—specifically in the mystery religion of Eleusis—rather than on Olympus, but whose ancient power has given way to the higher power of the brothers Hades and Zeus, as is clear in the story of the rape of Persephone told earlier.

Although the great goddess lost her position of dominance in European mythology, as in all Indo-European mythology with the possible exception of the Devī cults in India, her diminishment left a gap in the collective psyche that had to be filled. When the first Christian missionaries came to Europe, they unwittingly brought a gradually developing goddess myth that would eventually achieve hegemony there. This was a myth that would serve as both a culmination of the various European cultural goddess dreams and as at least a partial revival of the great goddess's power.

In the New Testament annunciation stories we are presented with the first aspect of the triune goddess—the goddess as sacred maiden. The maiden is impregnated by a divine being, but not, as with the Homeric hymn's Persephone, as the victim of rape. The New Testament maiden is more in the position of the Orphic Persephone who, as Zeus's daughter, is impregnated by her father as a serpent, the product being the god's son, Dionysos. The maiden, whose name is Mary or Miriam, agrees humbly to be the vessel for the emergence of the divine child, the *puer aeternus*, into the world. As such, she becomes part of an ancient mystery involving a triune god, whereby she is impregnated by God the Holy Spirit so she can give birth to God the Son and eventually reign in heaven with her son and God the Father.

Later gospel accounts depict Mary in her role as the second aspect of the triune goddess, the mother—protective, loving, and then grieving, like Baldr's mother, Frigg, over her son's death. The connection between the first and second aspects of the goddess are made abundantly clear in the many depictions in European art of the Virgin and child and the mother and the dead Christ (the Pietà).

The story of Mary as crone developed gradually in the apocryphal tradition of the early church in the Middle East and Europe. The church resisted her deification—"Let the Father, the Son and the Holy Spirit be worshipped," said one church father, "but let no one worship Mary" (Walker, 603)—and a Marianite sect that believed in Mary's divinity was persecuted in the early church. But Mary became in effect an immortal by way of the tradition and the eventual recognition by the church of her assumption bodily into heaven and of her place there as Theotokos, or mother of God, and de facto Queen of Heaven. The foundation of Mary's elevation was reinforced by the tradition and also late recognition by the church of her own sinlessness because of her immaculate conception. Conception without sin made possible her role as the New Eve in consort with the also immaculately conceived Christ, the New Adam.

Those who doubt the return of the goddess—a revived form of the Syrian Aphrodite-Mari, or Māyā the Buddha Mother, or the Egyptian Isis as Stella Maris (see Walker, 602)—albeit stripped of her essential sexuality, need only consider the great cathedrals of medieval Europe, frequently built over pagan sites and dedicated to the Blessed Virgin. The Virgin became for medieval Christians not only the representation of the church as an institution—the bride and holy mother of God—but an object of veneration and the primary receiver of prayer. Even her role as earth goddess was somewhat returned to her in her many European incarnations as the Black Madonna, the goddess of the dark and fertile earth or the dark phase of the moon from which light will come. Ean Begg, in *The Cult of the Black Virgin*, suggests that the Black Madonna was related to the ancient eastern fertility goddesses such as the Ionian Artemis, the Phrygian/Roman Cybele, and the Egyptian Isis, and that she was brought by the crusaders to western Europe (49).

Sky God

The pattern in European mythology that reflects the replacement of the Old Europe by the so-called Aryan or Indo-European culture is the emergence of a new power source no longer represented by earth-based deities but by the distinctly male sky gods. Like the ancient goddess that had three aspects and sometimes took form as three beings, the European supreme sky gods often were triadic within themselves or closely associated with two other gods. This arrangement followed the ancient Indo-European tradition of representing in the divine three functions—sovereign-priest, warrior, and cultivator-fecundator. In Rome the three qualities were represented by Jupiter, Mars, and Quirinus; among the continental Celts by Esus, Taranis, and Teutates; in Germanic Europe by Odin, Thor, and Freyr or Tyr; in the Baltic and Slavic areas by Perkuno in various combinations with other gods. A tendency toward the unification of the three functions is indicated in all of the European mythologies. Odin and Thor gained larger importance than Freyr or Tyr. Jupiter developed clearly as the supreme sky god in Rome, as did the thunder god among the Balts and Slavs. And this is certainly true from very early times in the person of Zeus in Greece. Zeus's very name reveals his dominance by way of his personification as the highest element, the sky. As has been mentioned, the proto-Indo-European equivalent of *Zeus* is *dyeus*, meaning sky. *Dyeus pater* is thus father sky; the Sanskrit is *dyaus* and *dyaus pita*. In the Indus Valley of India Dyaus, who in the earliest stories "covered" Pṛthvi (earth) as Ouranos covered Gaia in Greece, became Varuna in the Vedas, and in Persia, Ahura Mazda—all-seeing gods whose roots are in their being personifications of the sky. Thus, *Zeus* (Sky) *Pater* and in Rome *Ju Piter* (Jupiter).

As the combination of the principal roles of the tripartite godhead—sovereign, warrior, fecundator-storm god, priestly guardian of proper religious behavior that is dominated by the act of sacrifice—Zeus is a likely and logical predecessor for the Christian God. Developed from the Hebrew deity—this Christian God would complete his conquest of all Europe with the defeat in the late middle ages of the likes of Odin, Dievs, and Perkuno.

The Christian God contained within himself the tripartite arrangement of the earlier European gods and in fact, he incorporated the powers of all the deities in the various pantheons. His emergence in the early church as a trinity was almost inevitable. Like the old supreme gods he represented absolute and even arbitrary power. He was the wifeless god who created the world himself—*ex nihilo*—who killed the Egyptian first-born and drowned the Egyptian army in the Red Sea. It was he who tortured Job. He was, in short, the sovereign-warrior—the storm god who demanded sacrifice. But he was also the god who allowed a lamb to be substituted for Isaac in the sacrifice. And, it was this god, according to Christians, who chose to remain in heaven in his person as the Father, descending to earth as his Son to act as the ultimate sacrifice, and to remain there always as a spirit (translated as the Holy Ghost or Holy Spirit). He was creator-redeemer-sanctifier—three roles in one being. Or as Christian children learn, God is the Father, God is the Son, God is the Holy Spirit, but God the Father is not God the Son or God the Holy Spirit, God the Son is not God the Father or God the Holy Spirit, and God the Holy Spirit is not God the Father or God the Son. This theologically complex supreme being was the culmination of the Indo-European tripartite deity as it had developed in Europe.

The myth of the rise of Zeus to power in Greece tells us a great deal about the early stages of the post-Neolithic European god. The story—essentially the official creation story of the Olympian religion—is most fully told by Hesiod in his *Theogony*.

The Greek Creation

Hesiod tells us that in the beginning there was only chaos, that is the void, out of which came Gaia (mother earth) and Eros, or uncontrollable desire. Thus the feminine, although presumably stimulated by that uncontrollable urge, was still recognized as the source of the creation of the world. But in the Greek view, the mother quickly lost power to a stronger force. In fact, her first creation was Ouranos (Uranus), or sky—thus, the first of the patriarchal sky gods in Greece. Sky, of course, "covered" a now somewhat passive earth, reflecting, according to Robert Graves, the Hellenic invasion of the old goddess-based culture (1:32). And the offspring of this union included, among others, a number of many-headed monsters, the terrible single-eyed, thunder- and lightning-wielding Cyclopes, and, most importantly, the Titans among whom were Prometheus, Atlas, Themis (law), the earth goddess Rhea and Kronos (time).

Kronos hated his father, who hated him and all of Gaia's brood in return. Not wanting them to challenge him in daylight, Ouranos pushed each of his offspring into the depths of the great mother until she nearly exploded from her unnatural burden. In desperate rebellion against the violent power of her mate, Gaia made a sickle and challenged her children to use it against their father to achieve their freedom. It was Kronos who gladly took the opportunity to reach between earth and sky with the sickle and, by castrating his father, to achieve this early example of the common motif of the separation of the primal parents. Through this separation, room was made for light and life to thrive where there had been only darkness. When Kronos flung away his father's genitals, Gaia soaked up the resulting blood, which impregnated her with giants and with the vengeful Erinyes (Furies), chthonic female forces who would play havoc with the lives of the Greeks until they were tamed by the rational Olympians Apollo and Athena to become the Euemenides (Kind Ones). When Ouranos's genitals themselves landed in the ocean near Cyprus, the "foam" (semen) within them produced Aphrodite (later called a daughter of Zeus). The birth of this goddess, attended by Eros (later called her son), does not signify a return of goddess power. Goddesses such as Artemis and Athena would be masculinized by the Greeks, stripped of their earth-centered activities as deities of fertility, and removed to the sky god home of Mount Olympus as virginal Amazon-like warriors or huntresses. Aphrodite would be similarly associated in Greece not with the Indo-European ideal of sovereign power but with irrational passion. Hesiod tells us that her role was to stimulate the joys of love and the guiles that women employ to seduce men (59).

Back at the old home of Gaia, there was no revival of feminine dominance either. Instead, after the castration of Ouranos, Gaia *and* Ouranos became insignificant in the presence of the usurping and violent patriarchy represented by Kronos.

As abused children in adulthood often repeat the pattern of abuse, Kronos's approach to his children resembled his father's. Like Ouranos, he was a deity representing the sky. He mated with his sister Rhea, essentially a double of their mother, Gaia, as the embodiment of earth. The children of the union of Kronos and Rhea are the older generation of the familiar Olympian family discussed earlier: Hestia of the hearth; Demeter, the earth goddess and mother of Persephone; Hera, the often-wronged and nagging Queen of Olympus; Hades, the lord of the underworld and ravisher of his niece Persephone; Poseidon, the earth-shaking god of the seas; and Zeus, the thunder-sky god and patriarch.

But before achieving their ultimate stature and recognition, these children of Kronos were victims of their father's violence. As Kronos had usurped his father's throne, he worried that a son of his might do the same to him. His solution was to swallow each child immediately after birth. Rhea was overcome by grief and, ironically, begged for help from her elderly parents, the deposed Ouranos and Gaia. So it was that the pregnant Rhea was sent to Crete, and when the child Zeus was born, he was nursed there by Gaia, the ancient mother earth herself. Meanwhile Rhea substituted a stone wrapped in swaddling clothes for her newborn baby and fed it to Kronos. In this myth of Zeus's birth and nursing in Crete, we have a mythological conjunction of the old Minoan goddess culture and that of the invading Hellenes discussed in chapter 2.

The pain in Kronos's stomach that resulted from swallowing the stone was relieved by the act of vomiting suggested by the clever Rhea. Thus, not only the stone, placed near Delphi as a symbol of Zeus, but the swallowed offspring of Kronos and Rhea were released from their captivity in their father, Time. In gratitude, they gave their brother the hidden thunder and lightning, thereby recognizing him as the supreme sky god.

A great war in heaven followed the freeing of Kronos's off-spring. Kronos and the Titans were eventually defeated and imprisoned by Zeus and his brothers and sisters, with whom the Titan Prometheus allied himself. This was the Greek version of a nearly universal motif of war among the gods: the war between the Tuatha Dé Danaan and the Fomorians; the war between the Vanir and Aesir; Ragnarok, the end-of-the-world war between the gods and giants in the Norse Voluspa; the war between Lucifer and God in the Judeo-Christian tradition; the Armageddon of the Book of Revelation; and battles mirrored by epic human battles such as the one in the Indian *Mahābhārata* or Homer's *Iliad* are other versions.

Origins of Humanity

Various Greek stories describe the origins of humans. Some credit Zeus with the creation, others, Prometheus. Hesiod tells how Zeus created women to plague men as punishment for, among other things, having received the gift of fire from Prometheus (69–70).

The depiction of women as a curse finds expression in many Indo-European myths as well as in the biblical story of Adam and Eve. In this connection, it is significant that the Judeo-Christian God has no wife, unless Sophia, the sometimes female embodiment of wisdom, described by Gnostics and some philosophically minded Christians as God's eternal partner, is considered his wife. In any case, Sophia, particularly revered as Holy Wisdom by Eastern Christianity as indicated by the great cathedral of Saint Sophia in ancient Constantinople, was never a sexual being. In western Christianity her role as divine wisdom was in effect taken over by the third part of God as Holy Spirit.

The Judeo-Christian myth of creation tells how the universe was formless until the spirit of God moved over the waters. God then gradually spoke the world into existence over seven days and created humans in his image—first Adam and then, according to one of the Genesis stories, Eve from Adam's rib. When Adam and Eve sinned by eating forbidden fruit in the Garden of Eden, they brought death into the world and were exiled from paradise.

Sacrifice

In the Indo-European tradition, sacrifice is the essence of existence in an endless round of dissolution and renewal. The Vedic tradition of India tells of the Puruṣa, the first man, who is the universe past, present, and future, the object of the first sacrifice of existence. His mouth, out of which springs the primal syllable, is Brahman, the absolute or universal self, the essence that combines with nature to create reality at creation. The moon came from his consciousness and he knew himself, exclaiming "I Am." He is also Rudra (Śiva) who destroys the world in the ultimate sacrificial fire and Viṣṇu who reabsorbs reality into his own being. In the literal sense, Viṣṇu becomes the Purusa in the later Hindu myth of his self-decapitation by which he emerges as the primary god-sacrifice.

Norse mythology presents a clear example of the Puruṣa-like creation sacrifice.

The *Prose Edda* Creation

Basing his *Prose Edda* story primarily on the late tenth-century Eddic poem *Voluspa*, Snorri Sturluson tells of a strange creation derived from both fire and ice. In this myth, creation occurred between two entities that were already in existence—Muspell in the south and Niflheim in the north. Muspell was a place of fire where Black Surt with his flaming sword waited for his chance to destroy the world that would be created. Niflheim was a place of ice and snow, at the center of which was Hvergelmir, the spring from which the Elivagar, the eleven rivers, flowed. Between these two places was Ginnungagap, the great void into which the rivers poured, creating a desolate iciness in the north, which stood in contrast to equally desolate volcaniclike moltenness in the south. But in the middle of Ginnungagap, at the meeting of the two conflicting climates, was a mild area where melting ice became the evil frost giant Ymir. From under the left armpit of the sweating giant came a man and a woman. His legs came together to give birth to a family of frost giants. From the melting ice of the center, a cow called Audumla was born, and Ymir drank the four rivers of milk that poured from her. Audumla licked the ice for three days until a man named Buri appeared. Buri's son Bor married Bestla, the daughter of the frost giant Bolthor, and Bestla gave birth to the gods Odin, Vili, and Ve. As the de facto mother of the gods, Audumla seems to have roots in the Egyptian cow mother-goddess Hathor.

As they hated Ymir and the savage frost giants, the three sons of Bor killed Ymir. The great giant's spilled blood became a flood that drowned all of the frost giants with the exception of one Bergelmir and his wife, who escaped in a vessel made of a hollowed tree trunk. Then the three gods used Ymir's body to create the world: his flesh became earth, his bones became mountains and stones, his blood served well to make the lakes that dotted the world and the seas that surrounded it, and his skull was used for the sky. A dwarf stood at each of the four corners of the sky. The dwarfs were named East, West, North, and South. The gods made the sun and moon and stars from the sparks of Muspell. To the giants they assigned a place called Jotunheim. The three gods then created a protected and fertile area called Midgard from Ymir's eyebrows, and they created a man from a fallen ash tree and a woman from a fallen elm. Odin gave them life, Vili gave them intelligence and emotions, and Ve gave them senses. Ask was the man and Embla was the woman. These were the parents of the human race.

The similarity of elements of the Norse flood to those of the Sumerians, the Hebrews, and others suggests a common source, as does the familiar story of a dead primal god's body becoming an animistic world (Fee and Leeming, 140–1).

The Dying God

Sacrifice also takes mythological form in the many stories of the dying god. This motif exists outside of the Indo-European tradition as well as within it. In Sumer Inanna herself and her consort Dumuzi enact a ritual death and descent to the underworld, as does the goddess Hainuwele in Ceram, several African deities, and the great sacred god-king-priest Osiris in Egypt. In Europe there are several dying gods, or gods who undergo a ritual of death and renewal. The Norse god Odin, as we have seen, hangs himself on the world tree to learn the eternal truth of the runes. The Romans imported the year god Attis from Phrygia and practiced his rites of death and renewal in the spring. In Byelorussia and Russia we find the dying and reborn Iarilo, "god of heavenly light," who rides on a white horse and wears a crown of flowers.

Two pre-Christian dying god myths stand out in Europe. These are the myths of the Norse god Baldr—the beautiful god discussed earlier—and the Greek god Dionysos.

The Baldr myth that comes down to us by way of the *Prose Edda* and the work of Saxo Grammaticus may well have been influenced by the Christian tradition, but it seems to have existed in some form that predates that influence.

Dionysos, as indicated earlier, was the son of the supreme god Zeus by Persephone or Semele, depending on the source. The fact that Semele is a moon goddess is significant when we remember the association of the Vedic Puruṣa with the moon. Dionysos was said to have descended to the underworld in search of his mother. In another tradition, according to Robert Graves (1:57), he was a sacred king ritually killed and fed to his priestesses as sacred food. This is one version of his myth.

Zeus plucked him as a baby from the dead body of his lover, Semele,
all-too-mortal a woman, and the boy transformed himself into a lion,
a bull, and then a serpent (in echoing the three-part year). But no
disguise could long fool Hera, ever jealous of Zeus's philandery, ever
vengeful, who ordered the Titans to seize the little boy. They tore him
to pieces and boiled the gobbets in a cauldron. Where his blood had
fallen, a pomegranate tree grew, flowered, and fruited, its luscious
scarlet body holding a promising—and irresistible—profusion of
seeds.

Just so, his grandmother, Rhea, reconstituted him and brought him to
life again. He set out across the world, bearing his sacred vines. Re-
turning through Phrygia, he again encountered Rhea, who taught him
her holy mysteries of life and rebirth, and purified him.

Dionysos swept throughout Greece and the remainder of the world,
establishing his divinity among all people. He then ascended into
heaven and sat at the right hand of Zeus (Leeming and Page,
God, 99–101).

These mythologies indicate clearly that Europe was fertile
ground for the dying god from the east brought by Paul and
other missionaries. Jesus was at once priest, victim, king, and god.
As the Son of God, he was the ultimate sacrifice—the Purusa
who according to the missionaries was the Logos, who had always been and always would be. Through his sacrifice came eternal life. Like Odin on Yggdrasill, he hung on the tree—the world
tree or center of the universe being for Christians the cross, as
Delphi had been for the Greeks, or Saules Kok, the world tree of
the sun, for the Balts, the symbol of the meeting of time and
eternity—to confront the ultimate mystery of life and death.
Like Dionysos, he descended into hell in search of parents—in
this case the first parents, Adam and Eve. As Baldr's mother
grieved for her son, so Mary grieved for hers. Like Baldr, he was
a gentle and loving god. And like Dionysos he became, in the ceremony of bread and wine representing his body and blood, the

ritual food and drink of sacrifice, the new fruit on the new world tree who experienced dismemberment (symbolized by the spear wounds) and overcame death in resurrection.

The gospeler Matthew tells the story this way.

> *About daybreak on the first day of the week, when the Sabbath was over, Mary of Magdala and the other Mary came to look at the grave. Suddenly there was a violent earthquake; an angel of the Lord descended from heaven and came and rolled away the stone, and sat down on it. His face shone like lightning; his garments were white as snow. At the sight of him the guards shook with fear and fell to the ground as though dead.*
>
> *The angel spoke to the women: "You," he said, "have nothing to fear. I know you are looking for Jesus who was crucified. He is not here; he has been raised, as he said he would be. Come and see the place where he was laid, and then go quickly and tell his disciples: 'He has been raised from the dead and is going ahead of you into Galilee; there you will see him.' That is what I came to tell you."...*
>
> *The eleven disciples made their way to Galilee, to the mountain where Jesus had told them to meet him. When they saw him, they knelt in worship, though some were doubtful. Jesus came near and said to them: "Full authority in heaven and on earth has been committed to me. Go therefore to all nations and make them my disciples.... I will be with you always, to the end of time." (Matt. 28:1–7, 16–20)*

10

The European Mythic Hero

EROES BECOME IMPORTANT to cultures particularly when deities no longer come down to interact with us. Heroes—usually male in patriarchal cultures such as those of Europe—are often the offspring of the union of deities and mortals. To varying degrees they possess superhuman qualities, but they are also genuinely human like us. Achilles, Herakles, Odysseus, Cúchulainn, Sigurd, Lemminkäinen, and Beowulf are all heroes of European mythology whose powers come from some connection with divinity but who suffer the agonies and joys of human life. Heroes are our personae in the world of myth, expressions of our collective psyches, first as cultures and then as a species. Cúchulainn reflects the Irish physical and psychological experience and Achilles could not be anything else but Archaic Greek. But when we compare the heroes of these various cultures, Joseph Campbell's monomyth pattern emerges, and we discover a hero who belongs to the Indo-European tradition, to Europe, and ultimately to all of humanity.

The Monomyth

The hero's life sometimes begins with a clear sign of divine origin—a miraculous conception, a virgin birth, or some extraordinary childhood deed.

Herakles was conceived in the union between the disguised Zeus and a human woman, Alcmene, during a night that Zeus extended to the length of three nights in order to prolong his pleasure. (The hero Theseus was also conceived in such a union; in his case the god was Poseidon.) Zeus's wife, Hera, disapproving of the result of this act of infidelity, sent two great serpents to kill the baby in his crib, but the child gleefully strangled them both. His name, which means Hera's glory, was an attempt to placate the goddess. Hera agreed to allow Herakles to become a god if he could accomplish the famous twelve labors through which the hero would earn his name and represent the glory of Greece.

Divine Origins

Sigurd

The Germanic hero Sigurd (Siegfried), who figures prominently in the thirteenth-century *Volsunga Saga* in the north and in the German epic the *Nibelungenlied*, was thought to be of divine and human lineage. There are several childhood stories that speak to his heroic nature.

Sigurd, as several scholars have suggested, is the Arthur of the northern world and is perhaps based on a historical figure. He was mythologized in the sagas and was of German rather than Scandinavian origin. In the *Nibelungenlied*, he is the son of King Siegmund and Sieglinde. In the *Volsunga Saga*, he is the last of the Volsungs, the son of Sigmund, and was the only one of his family who could remove Odin's sword from Branstock, the oak. His mother was Hiordis. A tradition exists in which Sigurd's mother, threatened as a result of unfair accusations of infidelity, hid her newborn child in a bottle, which fell into the river and eventually broke on a shore. The child, Sigurd, was rescued by a doe and cared for by her for a year, by which time he had grown to the size of a four-year-old. One day he ran off into the forest, where he was rescued by the smith Mimir, who named and raised him. Before long, the boy performed miraculous deeds, revealing Herculean strength (Fee and Leeming, 119–20).

Cúchulainn

In Ireland it is sometimes difficult to distinguish heroes from gods. But out of the Ulster or Red Branch cycle, one great hero emerges in the person of Cúchulainn; the miraculous circumstances of his birth and initiation place him in the company of the multitude of heroes, including Zoroaster, Jesus, Herakles, and Theseus, whose beginnings are extraordinary.

> The mother of the hero-to-be was Dechtiré, the daughter of the druid Cathbad and the love god Aonghus. During the wedding feast of Dechtiré and the Ulster chieftain Sualtam, the god Lugh took the form of a mayfly and flew into the bride's drink. Dechtiré fell into a deep sleep, during which Lugh came to her in a dream and instructed her to leave with him, taking fifty maidens, whom he would disguise as birds. Nine months after the disappearance of the women, a group of hunting warriors followed a flock of birds to the river Boyne, thought to be the home of the gods. There they found a palace, where they were entertained by a handsome man and a beautiful woman surrounded by fifty maidens. During the night the woman gave birth to a boy. Lugh then revealed his own and Dechtiré's identity and instructed the hunters to return to Ulster with the mother and child and the maidens. There Sualtam welcomed back Dechtiré as his wife and the baby as his son.
>
> The child was first called Sétanta. But one day the king, Conchobhar, noticed the boy's prodigious strength and invited him to join him

at a feast being given by the smith Culann. There the smith's huge dog
attacked the child, who jammed his ball into the beast's mouth and
smashed its head against a rock, killing it instantly. Culann was furi-
ous that the child had killed his favorite watchdog, but Sétanta prom-
ised to find a replacement for the dog and until then to serve in its
place as the "Hound of Culann," or Cúchulainn (Fee and Leeming, 119).

The importance of superhuman powers and of the smith as a
guardian and namer thus figures in the stories of both Cúchulainn
and Sigurd and is reminiscent of similar patterns in the Greek
story of Oedipus and the Roman story of Romulus and Remus.

Arthur and the Sword from the Rock

Among the Celtic peoples of Britain, the Christianized Welsh King
Arthur is the most famous of heroes. His conception is at least un-
usual, and his initiation almost ritualistically follows the universal hero
pattern. As in ancient tales and Geoffrey of Monmouth's History of
the Kings of Britain, *Thomas Malory in the fifteenth-century* Le
Morte d'Arthur *has the magician Merlin tell Arthur the strange story*
of his conception.

According to that story, when Uther Pendragon (Uthr Bendragon)
was king of Britain, he was assisted in his wars against the invading
Saxons by the aging Duke of Cornwall. But Uther fell madly in love
with the duke's beautiful wife, Igraine, and made his love so evident
that the duke became offended and took his wife away to his castle at
Tintagel on the Cornish coast. As the castle was impregnable, Merlin
agreed to help Uther obtain Igraine. While the duke was away fight-
ing a battle, the magician used his magic to make Uther look like
Igraine's husband—so much so that the would-be lover was able to
enter the castle unchallenged and was admitted to Igraine's bed. That
night Arthur was conceived and the Duke of Cornwall was killed.

Merlin predicted that Igraine's child would be the greatest of the
kings of Britain. Eventually Igraine married Uther and Arthur was

born. It is said that elves attended the birth and that they gave the baby the gift of courage and strength, as well as intelligence, generosity, and longevity. When Uther asked Igraine who the child's father was, she admitted to having slept with a stranger who resembled her husband. Delighted by her honesty, Uther revealed that he was that stranger. For his own protection, the baby Arthur was given to Merlin, who gave him to Sir Ector to be raised.

When Uther Pendragon died, the British kingdom was threatened by dissent and disagreement. Realizing the danger, Merlin had the archbishop of Canterbury call together the nobles of the kingdom to decide who would be king. A stone with a sword in it suddenly appeared in a churchyard. These words were written on the stone: "Whoever pulls out this sword is the lawfully born king of Britain." At Christmas and again at New Year's, various nobles attempted without success to remove the sword. At that time, Arthur arrived at the stone with Sir Ector and his foster brother Sir Kay, whom he served as squire. Sir Kay asked Arthur to return to their camp to fetch a new sword for him. Arthur returned without having found one, but while passing by he noticed the sword in the stone, and while everyone was off at a tournament, he easily removed the sword from the stone and took it to Kay. Recognizing the sword, Kay decided to claim it and the throne. Sir Ector demanded to see for himself that his son could remove the sword from the stone. But when Kay replaced the sword in the stone he could not remove it. Moved by his father's questioning, he revealed that Arthur had given him the sword. When Arthur once again removed it from the rock, Sir Ector and Sir Kay knelt before him as their king. After much resistance, the nobles accepted Arthur as the lawful monarch, too, and Merlin revealed the details of his parentage (Fee and Leeming, 120–1).

The Quest

Once his identity is established, the hero typically embarks on an adventure. The adventure usually involves a search of some sort—for a parent, a talisman, or some essential knowledge or understanding. The questing hero is our cultural and collective psyche out on the edges of knowledge and existence. The adventurer is usually opposed by the forces of reaction, represented by dragons, femmes fatales, giants, and the powers of death itself, into the depths of which the hero often descends before, like his dying-god antecedents, he miraculously returns.

Herakles accomplishes his labors, descends to the underworld, and returns. Theseus removes his human father's shoes from under the rock and goes in search of him. He also descends to the underworld and returns, as does the Roman Aeneas who leaves the burning Troy in search of the new Troy, Rome. All of these heroes face and overcome monsters and temptations. All of them are superhuman, but all of them reveal human foibles, the chief one being their mortality. The Anglo-Saxon Beowulf descends to the depths to defeat the mother of the monster Grendel and ends his life fighting the great dragon. Sigurd, too, is a dragon fighter.

Sigurd the Dragon Slayer

After Odin, Loki, and Hoenir had paid Otter's ransom to Hreidmar and his sons with Andvari's tainted gold, the kin of Otter fell out over the division of this wergild. Regin and Fafnir, Hreidmar's two remaining sons, wished to have their shares immediately. Their father refused them, however, and as a result Fafnir killed his father in his sleep and made off into the barren wilds with his ill-gotten loot; there he transformed himself into a great venomous serpent, and he spent his life brooding over his cursed treasure and laying waste the countryside all around. Regin, meanwhile, left penniless, went to the court of King Hjalprek, where he worked as a smith. After the birth of Sigurd, Regin served as his foster father, raising the boy in his household and teaching him the pastimes of nobility and the mystery of runes. As Sigurd began to grow to manhood, his foster father attempted to incite in him the pride and heroic spirit necessary to confront Fafnir. Eventually Sigurd agreed to the confrontation on the condition that Regin forge for him a magnificent sword. Regin created two lesser blades that Sigurd shattered upon the anvil, but the third time Sigurd bade him use the two pieces of Sigmund's broken blade that Sigurd had obtained from his mother as his inheritance. This blade was named Gram, and when Regin had refashioned it, it cut easily through the anvil. Sigurd now agreed to face Fafnir, once he had avenged his own father's death.

Once Sigurd had accomplished this vengeance, he returned to Regin and prepared to make good his oath. They traveled together to the heath upon which Fafnir lived and searched until they found the track leading from the lair of the worm to his watering hole. Regin advised Sigurd to dig a trench across this track, to lie in wait within the trench until Fafnir crossed over it, and then to thrust his sword into the serpent's heart. Sigurd asked what would happen to him if he were submerged in the dragon's blood, but Regin merely derided him for his cowardice and made off in haste. Sigurd dug a trench as he had been told, but before he had finished an old gray-bearded wanderer appeared before him and noted that he should dig a series of drainage trenches so that he would not come to harm from the worm's blood. This old wanderer then vanished; it was not the first time the young hero had been helped by the all-seeing one.

Having completed his task, Sigurd hid himself at the bottom of the central trench; he had not long to wait. Soon the earth trembled with the approach of the dragon, and poison spewed all around; but Sigurd was safe in his hiding place. Just as the belly of the beast passed over him, Sigurd thrust the sword with all his might through the heart of the evil one, and thus the serpent received its death blow. Fafnir asked who had slain him and why, but at first Sigurd refused to reveal his identity; finally, however, stung by the taunts of the dying beast, Sigurd foolishly revealed his name, and so the dragon was able to pass the curse of the gold along to his killer. Sigurd did not fear death, however, and so determined to take the gold anyway and be rich until the day marked out for his fall. After Sigurd had interrogated Fafnir concerning his wisdom about the gods, the dragon died.

*With his vile kin safely put to rest, Regin soon appeared on the scene
and demanded his share of Otter's wergild, denied to him for so long:
Sigurd might keep all the hoard, but Regin asked of the warrior the tri-
fle of Fafnir's roasted heart. This request Sigurd granted, and then
Regin drank of the serpent's blood and fell into a deep sleep. While
Regin slumbered, Sigurd roasted the dragon's heart for him. Burning
his finger by accident, however, Sigurd thrust his digit into his mouth.
Upon tasting the blood of the worm, Sigurd suddenly found himself
able to understand the speech of birds and learned from those around
him of Regin's plotted treachery against him. Determining now to
send one brother upon the heels of the other, Sigurd drew Gram once
more and took his false-hearted foster father's head. Then he ate some
of the heart of Fafnir and packed the rest away. Finally Sigurd made
his way to the lair of the dragon, gathered up all of the treasure he
found there, and left to seek the shield-maiden Brynhild* (Fee and
Leeming, 130–1).

Cúchulainn and the *Táin Bó Cuailnge*

*One of the greatest of the European cultural heroes is Cúchulainn,
whose exploits are central to the Irish epic the* Táin Bó Cuailnge.
The Táin *concerns Queen Medb's (Maeve) attempt to capture the
Brown Bull of Cuailnge. The bull itself is a highly symbolic animal in
Irish myth. It stands, as it does in most ancient Indo-European cultures, for power and virility and is associated in Ireland especially
with sacred kingship. According to the* Book of the Dun Cow, *the
election of the Irish king was marked by a ceremony in which a druid
ate a bull's flesh and drank its blood and then, in a deep sleep,
dreamed of the future king.*

The great war of the Táin *developed out of a pillow-talk argument
between Medb and Ailill over the relative value of their possessions.
(Zeus and Hera had such arguments and so did the Indian god Śiva
and his wife, Pārvatī.) When Medb realized that her possessions were
inferior to her husband's, owing to his ownership of Finnbennach, the
White-horned Bull, she determined to obtain for herself Donn Cuail-*

nge, the great Brown Bull of Cuailnge. This bull could engender fifty calves in a day and could carry fifty boys on its back. It could shelter a hundred warriors with its body. The two bulls had once possessed human form as swineherds: one served the king of Connaught, the other, the king of Munster. The two swineherds, once friends, had become jealous of each other and had fought over the relative values of their herds. In these fights they had taken various forms—warriors, ravens, and monsters. Finally they changed themselves into maggots, and one swam into a river in Cuailnge and was swallowed by a cow belonging to the Ulster chieftain Daire. The other swam into a Connaught stream and was consumed by one of Queen Medb's cows. The former swineherds were reborn as the White-horned Bull of Connaught and the Brown Bull of Cuailnge.

Medb asked Daire for the loan of the Brown Bull for a year, and Daire agreed until it was reported to him that the wily queen's ambassadors had boasted that if the loan had been refused, she would have taken the bull by force anyway. Here the ancient Indo-European theme of the cattle theft is expressed. Daire rescinded his agreement to the loan, and an enraged Medb prepared for war, engaging the exiled former Ulster king Fergus as her general. Fergus hated Conchobhar because of an earlier betrayal involving Fergus's honor. But he remained loyal in spirit to his "foster son," the Ulster hero Cúchulainn, and warned him of the impending war.

Medb assumed that because of a curse that had enfeebled the Ulstermen, victory for Connaught would be a simple matter. But she had not reckoned on the fact that Cúchulainn was not by birth an Ulsterman. When Medb attacked Ulster, she was confronted by Cúchulainn in his war chariot driven by the faithful Laig (Laeg) and drawn by the greatest of war horses, the Battle Gray. The slingshot of Cúchulainn was a deadly weapon, and before long countless Connaught warriors lay dead. Amazed by the prowess of this mere seventeen-year-old, Medb determined to meet him and hoped to bring him over to her side with her charms. After much haggling, Medb and Cúchulainn agreed that from then on Cúchulainn would *fight in daily single combat any warrior sent to him. The Connaught army might advance for only as long as it took him to defeat his daily enemy. While Cúchulainn defeated warrior after warrior with ease, allowing Medb's army only marginal advances, the devious queen took advantage of the hero's preoccupation by stealing the Brown Bull.*

Now the gods had been watching Cúchulainn's amazing feats of battle and the war goddess Mórrigán, especially, had noticed his prowess. Appearing to the hero in a red dress and riding in a red war chariot, the goddess attempted to seduce him. (She thus resembled the great Inanna who practiced her wiles on the hero of the Sumerian-Babylonian epic, Gilgamesh.) Claiming that it was she who had made his victories possible, Mórrigán demanded repayment in the form of love. When Cúchulainn rashly claimed he needed no woman's help in battle and reacted disdainfully to the goddess's charms, she became his mortal enemy and made his tragic fate inevitable.

Soon Medb sent the old warrior Loch out to fight with Cúchulainn at what became ever after a famous ford. Loch was assisted by Mórrigán in the form of a heifer, an eel, and a wolf, each of which Cúchulainn defeated. But Loch was able to inflict many wounds on his enemy, and the combination of warrior and goddess was about to prevail when Cúchulainn decided, reluctantly, since he considered such tactics dishonorable, to make use of his magical spear, the Gae Bolga, a weapon against which there was no defense. Loch was thus killed. The much-wounded Cúchulainn was given a strong sleeping potion by his true father, the god Lugh, and during three days and nights of sleep was cured by the ministration of the god's powerful medicine.

Sensing impending defeat, Medb now insisted that Fergus himself fight Cúchulainn. A battle with the youth he considered his "foster son" was anathema to the former Ulster king. Finally, after Medb called him a coward Fergus agreed to fight, but only without the assistance of his famous invincible sword. As the two friends and great warriors approached each other, they tried to find a way to avoid the fight. Finally they agreed that Cúchulainn should pretend to run from Fergus in fear on the condition that in a similar situation in the future Fergus would run from Cúchulainn. As Cúchulainn ran away after a pretend battle, the forces of Medb mocked him.

Now Medb decided to put an end to Cúchulainn even if that meant breaking her oath of single combat only. She sent the wizard Calatin with his 27 sons to fight her enemy. It was only with the help of Fiacha, another Ulster exile sent by Fergus to watch the battle, that Cúchulainn was able to destroy the wizard and his children.

With her next ploy, Medb was almost successful. Against Cúchulainn she sent Ferdia of the impenetrable skin, a childhood friend of the great hero. The two had sworn eternal friendship, and it was only the threats to their reputations and honor that led them to fight each other. The two fought for three days, and each night Cúchulainn demonstrated his love by sharing the medicine of Lugh to cure Ferdia's wounds. Finally, the anger of battle prevailed, and Cúchulainn once again made reluctant use of the Gae Bolga, as Karṇa made use of a magical weapon in the Indian epic the Mahābhārata and King Arthur wielded the magic sword Excalibur. As Ferdia died at his feet, Cúchulainn moaned in agony at the loss of his friend.

The battle with Ferdia had left Cúchulainn badly wounded. Unable to continue the war alone, he sent his adopted father Sualtam, who had come to nurse his wounds, to ride to Ulster on the Battle Gray to call on the Ulstermen for help. It was only when Sualtam's severed head—which was cut off by his shield as a result of the abrupt movement of Cúchulainn's horse—continued to cry out the call for help that the Ulstermen arose from their long, curse-induced stupor and sent an army to aid their hero. The speaking severed head is a common motif in Celtic myth.

When the forces of Conchobhar approached those of Medb, Cúchulainn revived, and he joined them. Facing Fergus, he demanded that his old friend fulfill his part of the oath of retreat, and Fergus turned and ran, causing havoc in his own army, which fled in disarray. The battle was thus won, but the Brown Bull remained in Con-

*naught, and his old hatred of the White-horned Bull revived. A great
battle of the bulls resulted, and eventually the Brown Bull defeated his
enemy, essentially dismembered him, and with much bellowing, returned to Cuailnge, where soon his heart burst and he died.*

*As for Cúchulainn, his doom was manipulated by the witch daughters
of the enchanter Calatin and by the young kings of Munster and Leinster, whose fathers—as well as the father of the witches—Cúchulainn had slain in battle. And, of course, the offended Mórrigán was
an interested party in her enemy's destruction. The witches used their
magic to lure Cúchulainn out with only the horse the Battle Gray and
the charioteer Laig. In spite of terrible omens, Cúchulainn insisted on
venturing toward the standing Pillar of Stone. There he met the three
witches and was taunted by three bards, who used threats of poetic
dishonor to cause the hero to throw his three spears at them. The
bards thus were killed, but Lughaid, king of Munster, and Erc, king
of Leinster, threw the spears back at Cúchulainn, first killing Laig,
then the Battle Gray, and then wounding Cúchulainn in his guts.
The dying hero struggled to the pillar stone and tied himself to it so
that he might die standing. At this moment Mórrigán arrived as a
crow and sat proudly on the dying man's shoulder, and Lughaid cut
off his head. The hero's falling sword severed Lughaid's arm, however, and soon Cúchulainn's friend Conall would sever Lughaid's
head to avenge the unfair defeat of the greatest of Irish heroes* (Fee
and Leeming, 172–5).

The Once and Future King

King Arthur's heroic quest is undertaken by his Knights of the
Round Table—Percival, Gawain, and others who, among other
adventures, seek the holy grail, the cup used by Jesus at the Last
Supper. Although in all likelihood he had pagan roots, Arthur is
one of many warrior heroes—Roland of the *Song of Roland*, Joan
of Arc, El Cid of the great Spanish national epic—are others
who emerged from the establishment of Christianity in Europe.
In fact, the pagan heroes were all assimilated in one way or an-

other by the retelling of their stories by Christian writers such as the *Beowulf* poet and Snorri Sturluson in the north. Central to the King Arthur myth is his role as the "once and future king" who, although dead would return one day. In this role, Arthur follows the monomyth model of the hero's return from the depths and, specifically, of Jesus, who went to heaven with the promise of returning one day in glory.

> *In 1113, some French clergy visited Bodmin near Dartmoor in Cornwall in search of Arthurian sites. There they learned of the Cornish-Breton tradition that King Arthur, who some said had been killed by his son or nephew Mordred (Modred) in battle, was in fact alive, as prophesied by the magician Merlin. It was believed that he had been wounded and taken away to be cured by certain fairy queens—some say by his sister, the enchantress Morgan Le Fay—to the mysterious island of Avallon (Avalon), called the Isle of Apples by Geoffrey of Monmouth and the Isle of Women in older Celtic tradition, from which place he will one day return to save Britain. In Sicily a story developed of Arthur's remaining forever young because he was fed from the holy grail. In many places Arthur was associated with the strange figure of the fisher-king, whose wounds are somehow tied to the physical and spiritual fertility of the land. In the early thirteenth century, Gervase of Tilbury supported this association by asserting that Arthur's wounds reopened each year. These and many other stories are part of the popular belief in a de facto apotheosis, or deification, of the "once and future king"* (Fee and Leeming, 136).

Jesus

The development of the Christian hero was a natural outgrowth of the Christian hegemony achieved throughout the continent during the first millennium c.e. The essential hero myth or monomyth inevitably found new clothes in the new religion that combined several basic elements: the teachings and activities of a Jewish reformer whose life story or hero mythology was affected

by borrowings from older mythologies of the Middle East; traditions developed in the various primarily but not exclusively
Indo-European mythological systems and philosophies of the
European tribes; and a full development of the archetypal patterns of the monomyth, patterns familiar to the human psyche
in general. What we know as European Christianity has always,
of course, been marked by internal divisions traceable in part to
the old cultural differences. These divisions have been extreme in
a history that has included the East-West split of the old Roman
Empire and the later rise of Protestantism, not to mention
purely political and economic differences. But, the essential elements of the *mythological* hero construct underlying the various
versions of Christianity—regardless of ritualistic, doctrinal, and
governing systems—have remained constant.

As Zeus and the other great sky gods were absorbed into the
Christian God and Mary successfully replaced the great goddess,
Jesus gathered together in himself not only the elements of the
dying god myth noted above but those of the old European hero
myth. To Greeks, Romans, Slavs, Celts, Germans, and Scandinavians listening to the Christian missionaries, the myth of Jesus
would not have been much of a surprise. It would have sounded
like this.

Jesus was miraculously conceived when his mother-to-be—a
young woman named Mary betrothed to a carpenter—was impregnated by God in his Holy Spirit aspect. As a child, his importance was revealed by a visit of astrologers from the east who saw
him as a king. Somewhat later he proved himself in the temple of
his religion by demonstrating divine wisdom beyond his years. In
certain texts known as the apocryphal or noncanonical gospels, we
are told that as a child in Egypt, where his family had taken him to
avoid the monstrous King Herod, he picked some ears of corn,
ate the kernels from them, and later the field "yielded so many
measures of wheat as the number of grains he had taken in." He
also turned salted fish into living fish (Leeming/Page, *God*, 93).

Jesus then left home, was tempted by the devil, and went on to perform numerous Herculean miracles such as raising the dead and curing diseases. After instructing his followers on how to remember him in a sacrificial ceremony, he was hanged on a cross, died there, descended to the underworld to again confront the monstrous devil, and he returned as a living being before ascending on a cloud up to the supreme being.

It was this myth that superseded all other hero myths of the pre-Christian ages and spawned the subsidiary Christian hero myths such as those mentioned above. Through it Europe became *mythologically* a single entity, paying lip service even to the new message brought by the new hero, a message that sounded more like the message of the eastern Buddha than that of the old European heroes. In terms of practice, from the Crusades to modern wars, Europeans have tended to attach the values of the old heroes—military dominance and cultural differentiation and power—to a hero who clearly decried such values and whose truer representatives were the martyrs and saints—Francis, Brigid, Patrick, and others—known more for their missionary work, self-sacrifice, and humility than for military skill.

So it is that a host of European-based cultural "myths" has developed directly or indirectly from Christian hegemony in the continent and a perversion of the original Christian myth. If romantic notions of chivalry grew in part out of veneration of "Our Lady," the Virgin Mary, the prevailing belief in the exclusive rightness of the dominant religion led to the hierarchical, male-dominated traditions of the European church along with such insidious offshoots as the Inquisition, inherent anti-semitism, the concept of paganism attached to other religions, the theory of the divine right of kings, and the Crusades. In America myths of manifest destiny and the self-made man grew out of European Calvinist doctrines of predestination and, when attached to European Darwinian views of natural selection, were used to justify the conquest of indigenous peoples, the suppression of the working poor, and the decimation of nature. A general sense of European or white superiority was used to justify European colonialism and the literal or virtual enslavement of nonwhites, and even, by way of a new Aryan myth supported as well by the perversion of pre-Christian Germanic mythology, the genocidal horrors of Nazism. Christian millennialism and messianic beliefs can be said to have provided ripe ground for the utopian myth that underlay European communism, which itself was easily misdirected, as the European church had been, to a hierarchical totalitarianism.

Finally, the old Judeo-Christian mythology may be said to have spawned much of what we know as modern economics, in part by way of Adam Smith's "invisible hand," the mysterious mechanism and metaphorical substitute for the old supreme being that he described in *The Wealth of Nations* as the controlling force behind economic activity. The invisible hand can be said to have given birth in turn to a current mythological figure of immense power, the market, to which has been attributed, by its theoretical "priests" and governments everywhere, the ability to decide what is best for us even in areas once left to other, at least sometimes more human and humane, arbiters of well-being and morality. This economic mythology can be said to be the driving power behind not only European conservative movements but the whole concept of a unification of Europe, which neither the old pagan gods nor the God and heroes of Christianity nor the totalitarian myths of the twentieth century could achieve.

11

European Philosophical Myths
and the Modern World

A N IMPORTANT TYPE of myth since Plato's time has been the metaphorical tale used to explain realities that are beyond simple logic. These "philosophical myths," of which Adam Smith's "invisible hand" is one, differ radically from most of the myths discussed earlier in this book, because they are constructs of individuals rather than of collective entities such as cultures, nations, movements, and the species. Several European philosophical myths should be mentioned here as they have profoundly affected the way Europeans and others see themselves in relation to the world they inhabit.

Plato's Cave

Plato himself was fond of creating such myths, of which his most famous is the so-called Myth of the Cave, found in the sixth book of the *Republic*.

Plato describes an eternal and constant reality from which humankind has become isolated but with which reunion is possible. In the myth of the cave, our world is seen as merely a shadow of what Plato's follower Plotinus (205–270 C.E.) called the One from which existence emanates. Plato suggests that we imagine some men who have lived since childhood in a place underground that can only be reached by way of a tunnel-like passage that eventually opens to the light. Since the men are chained by the neck, they can only see what lies in front of them. Above and behind them is a fire that creates light, and between them and the fire there is a track with a wall below it. The wall serves to hide people behind it, much as puppeteers are hidden in a puppet show. These people move objects that appear on the track above them. The objects are representations of animals, inanimate figures, humans, and so forth. The prisoners cannot see the fire, the wall, or the track. They can only see the shadows on the wall in front of them caused by the objects and the firelight behind them. When the people behind the wall give voices to the models they move, the prisoners hear only the echoes of those voices. Plato says that the condition of the prisoners represents our own position in relation to the light outside the cave. Like us, they are separated from the source of being and are doomed to see only shadows of being until such time as they can achieve enlightenment (see Leeming, *Myth*, 43–4).

Myths of God

Various philosophical myths have been created to explain God. One of the most important in terms of its influence on later theology is that of Aristotle. When considering nature, Aristotle sees an orderly system motivated and directed by a substance beyond nature, a supreme "unmoved mover"—in other words, by God. Everything in nature tries to imitate God. Aristotle's view of God did much to make Europe a fertile ground for the later planting of the Christian concept of God.

A myth developed by the Russian mystic and philosopher Vladimir Solov'ev envisions God as ultimate reality in gradual union with creation by way of the relationship between the

Logos—the word, or essence of active creation—and Sophia, feminine and passive divine wisdom and bride of the Christ as the Logos.

Another philosophical myth of God is the eighteenth-century deistic one that saw the unmoved mover as a kind of clockmaker, who built the clock (the world) at the creation, wound it up, and left it to run on its own. This was the essentially nonpersonal God of many of the great thinkers of the Age of Reason whom we describe as deists (as opposed to theists). It was a vision that greatly affected the thinking of many of the European-bred founding fathers of the United States and perhaps contributed to the separation of church and state that has been so important for the American social and political experience.

Psychological Myths

Most myths are stories with definable characters and events. These characteristics apply to the philosophical myth that perhaps had more influence on the way twentieth-century people thought of themselves and regarded the world around them than the religious myths that preceded it. The myth in question, developed primarily by an Austrian doctor, Sigmund Freud, is literally a part of our vocabulary and our prevailing belief system. It begins with the concept of the unconscious, the psyche, an entity that, as the gospeler John said of God and might have said of an analogous entity, the soul, "no man hath seen." Freud's psyche comes with popularly accepted characters: the elemental urge-driven Id, the moralistic and controlling Superego, and the heroic Ego who must achieve balance between all of the psychic elements. Freud is concerned with such mythic events as the Oedipus or Elektra complexes, which take their names in turn from ancient myth, and such concepts as the primal horde in which fathers deny their sons sexual access to the females of their clans.

The psychological myth was further developed by the Swiss

psychiatrist and philosopher Carl Jung and others. Jung, especially, not only made extensive use of ancient myth as cultural dream in his clinical work, but added a host of characters to the philosophical myth—such as the Anima and Animus (the projection onto the opposite sex of the individual's psychic energy or true inner self), the Self (the Egolike mediator between the conscious and unconscious worlds), and the Shadow (the negative side of the personality). In Jung's version of the myth, the individual as Self enters into something very like a heroic journey-quest with the support of his Anima and the opposition of his Shadow. The goal is self-identity or individuation, a mythic goal that many twentieth-century and early twenty-first-century people believe in implicitly, as indicated by their willingness to pay a great deal of money for guides (psychotherapists) who can help them on their way.

The perils of the psychological journey-quest, whether with a Freudian, Jungian, or other sort of guide, are as real as those facing the old mythic hero. This is a dark night of the soul, or a night journey fraught with monsters to be overcome, pitfalls to be avoided. In this it reminds us of Theseus's journey to his father, Odysseus's ten-year voyage from Troy to Ithaca, or that great Christian philosophical journey myth contained in Dante's *Divine Comedy*, in which the human persona must descend to the depths of human sin and depravity, guided by the wise Vergil, before he may begin the upward journey to God.

Scientific Myths

The physicists of our time, like Plato and Aristotle before them, and like their colleagues in psychology, have turned to philosophical myth to explain the reality they believe they have discovered. They make use of myth—of stories with characters— because the majority of people are to a great extent ignorant of what is, in effect, the sacred and secret language of physics, mathematics. Physicist Erwin Schrödinger's famous "Cat in the Box" thought experiment is one such myth.

> In a box there is some radioactive material, an atom of which has a 50 percent chance of decaying in a set time and being recorded by a detector. There is also a live cat and a container of poison in the box. If the atom decay does not occur, the container will break and the cat will die. There is seemingly a 50 percent chance that after a certain time the cat in the box will be dead. So, we know after a while that the cat is either dead or alive. But, in the world of quantum mechanics this logic does not apply. According to that world, the cat cannot be either dead or alive until we actually open the box to see what has happened. Only through conscious observation does anything become real (Leeming, Myth, 17).

There are many such myths and there will be many more. Europeans, like other humans, continue to be myth makers, telling stories to reveal what they see around them and to hypothesize about the past and future. No one, for instance, was present at the beginning of time, but the stories of the big-bang creation and evolution are now as generally accepted as the story of Gaia and Ouranos once was in Greece. There is as much unwillingness to apply the word "myth" to these concepts as there once was to apply it to the tale of Genesis or the ascension of Jesus.

A thought model devised in part by a British-European scientist named James Lovelock points both to the power of the old myths and the emergence of the new (Lovelock, 12). Lovelock's Gaia hypothesis, takes its name from the Greek creatrix, the mother earth goddess herself. It is a model, informed, for example, by the narratives that are thermodynamics, the big bang, and evolution. It speaks, like most myth, to human tragedy and to what might be called universal or ultimate hope. It is a philosophical myth that expresses our era's discovered reality, that in spite of its division and wars, Europe is much more importantly an ecological unity, as is, for that matter, the whole world. As a myth, Lovelock's hypothesis might sound like this:

Imagine a world called Daisyworld.

Daisyworld supports life in the simple form of black daisies and white daisies. Early on in the planet's existence, the sun was faint and weak (as it once was on our planet). Since the black daisies were better at absorbing the weak radiation of the sun and using it to grow, they dominated the planet. Daisyworld's surface was mostly black.

But as time passed, the sun gave off more and more energy as it aged (as our sun is doing). The black daisies that covered most of the planet absorbed more and more heat until it became too hot for black daisies to thrive.

Meanwhile, the few white daisies that had managed to survive on this planet reflected more heat than they absorbed and thus did poorly in cooler times, but they were more comfortable when the sun gained strength. Soon, white daisies spread while black ones shrank in terri-tory, and with more white daisies, the planet's surface as a whole began to cool.

The black-white, heat absorption-reflection process is like a thermo-stat that keeps the heat level right for daisies in general (i.e., life) to flourish. If too many white daisies were to grow, it would get too cool, and the black daisies would do better and expand ... and so on.

Of course, conditions on earth are far more complicated than those on Daisyworld. But scientists must study such systems on earth, in part because of fears of the greenhouse effect, the potential heating of the earth by a rapid build-up of gases like carbon dioxide (which tend to let the sun's heat in and keep the earth's heat from escaping). Meanwhile, clouds tend to have the opposite effect, reflecting solar radiation away from the earth and thus cooling it. And more and more evidence is accumulating that life—especially in the form of tiny creatures like bacteria and the ocean's plankton (tiny floating larvae and microscopic beings)—plays a direct and continuing role in the

*global carbon dioxide budget, the cloud cover, and other factors that
are, or may be, at work in the atmosphere.*

*Indeed, so important is the role of life forms such as bacteria, it may
be that the true function of large animals, such as mammals (including, of course, humans), is to provide comfortable habitats for bacteria in their guts.*

*The Gaia hypothesis, whether true or not, is helpful in reminding us
that there is more to life than merely us humans. Those who are
rightly concerned with humanity must also be concerned for their
lesser companions.*

*We are, Lovelock has said, bound to be eaten, for Gaia customar-
ily eats her children. What is certain is death and decay, which seems
a small price to pay for life. The price of an identity in life is mortality. Families live longer than individuals, tribes longer than families,
species longer than tribes, and so on.*

*But all will one day go from here forever, as the sun ages and dies in
a searing inferno. And life may, or may not, find another abiding
place in this, or another universe* (Leeming and Page, *Goddess*,
175–6).

Ultimately, myths are necessary for our psychic well-being. They
tell the story of existence as far as existence can be understood at
any given time. The myth of Europe is, like Europe itself, still
evolving; Europeans are still trying to tell their story, still trying
to understand and articulate what it means to be at once individual cultures and a unified people in more than a merely geographical sense. The Christian myth moved Europe toward a unified and defining mythology beginning early in the first
millennium C.E., but cultural differences indicated by older myths
have taken precedence over that myth and Europe has been
scarred by nearly continuous wars between its tribes since the advent of Christianity. And now Europe is experiencing realities
that neither the Christian nor the so-called pagan or ethnic myths
can encompass. Religious and cultural diversity has increased

rather than decreased in recent times, and the myths of psychology, science, and geopolitics, along with realities of economics
and ecology, have challenged Europeans to find a new way to de-
fine themselves. It may well be that any new European myth
would, in any case, be superfluous in the face of larger global realities and interconnections. In fact, it may be that Europeans
and non-Europeans alike, even as they celebrate the various levels
of their identifying cultural differences, must move beyond those
differences, those cultural dreams, to a realization that in a global
community such as ours, exclusive cultural entities, whether religious, ethnic, national, or continental, must give way to the larger
needs of Gaia.

Bibliography

Armstrong, Karen. *A History of God*. New York: Alfred Knopf, 1993.
Backman, Louise. "Saami Religion." In *The Encyclopedia of Religion*, ed. Mircea Eliade, 12:497–9. New York: Macmillan, 1987.
Baring, Anne, and Jules Cashford. *The Myth of the Goddess: Evolution of an Image*. London: Penguin, 1993.
Begg, Ean. *The Cult of the Black Virgin*. London: Arkana, Routledge & Kegan Paul, 1985.
Bierlein, John Francis. *Parallel Myths*. New York: Ballantine Books, 1994.
Biezais, Haralds. "Baltic Religion." In *The Encyclopedia of Religion*, ed. Mircea Eliade, 2:49–55. New York: Macmillan, 1987.
Blazquez, Jose M. "Basque Religion," trans. Erica Melzer. In *The Encyclopedia of Religion*, ed. Mircea Eliade, 2:80–81. New York: Macmillan, 1987.
———. "Iberian Religion." In *The Encyclopedia of Religion*, ed. Mircea Eliade, 6:547–51. New York: Macmillan, 1987.
Bloch, Raymond. "Etruscan Religion," trans. Carol Dean-Nassau and Marilyn Gaddis Rose. In *The Encyclopedia of Religion*, ed. Mircea Eliade, 5:182–5. New York: Macmillan, 1987.
Boer, Charles, trans. *The Homeric Hymns*. Chicago: Swallow Press, 1970.
Bonnefoy, Yves. *Asian Mythologies*. Ed. Wendy Doniger. Chicago: University of Chicago Press, 1993.
———. *Roman and European Mythologies*. Ed. Wendy Doniger. Chicago: University of Chicago Press, 1991.
Bowker, John, ed. *The Oxford Dictionary of World Religions*. New York and Oxford: Oxford University Press, 1997.
Branston, Brian. *Gods of the North*. New York: Thames and Hudson, 1955, 1980.
Caesar, Julius. See Hammonds.

Campbell, Joseph. *The Hero with a Thousand Faces* (1949). Princeton: Princeton University Press, 1972.

————. *The Masks of God: Creative Mythology* (1968). New York: Viking, 1970.

————. *The Masks of God: Occidental Mythology* (1964). New York: Viking, 1970.

————. *The Masks of God: Oriental Mythology* (1962). New York: Viking, 1970.

————. *The Masks of God: Primitive Mythology* (1969). New York: Viking, 1970.

————. *The Way of the Animal Powers.* London: Summerfield Press, 1983.

Chadwick, Nora K., ed. *The Celts.* New York: Penguin Books, 1997.

Cicero, See Rudd.

Crossley-Holland, Kevin. *The Norse Myths.* New York: Pantheon, 1980.

Culiano, Ioan Petru, and Cicerone Poghirc. "Thracian Religion." In *The Encyclopedia of Religion,* ed. Mircea Eliade, 14:494–7. New York: Macmillan, 1987.

Cunliffe, Barry. *The Ancient Celts.* New York: Oxford University Press, 1997.

Davidson, Hilda Roderick Ellis. *Gods and Myths of Northern Europe.* Harmondsworth, U.K.: Penguin, 1964.

————. *Roles of the Northern Goddess.* New York: Routledge, 1998.

———— and Peter Fisher, trans. *Saxo Grammaticus: The History of the Danes.* Woodbridge, U.K.: Boydell & Brewer, 2001.

Davies, Paul. *The New Physics.* New York and Cambridge: Cambridge University Press, 1989.

De Voragine, Jacobus. *The Golden Legend.* London: Longmans, Green, 1941.

Domotor, Tekla. "Hungarian Religion." In *The Encyclopedia of Religion,* ed. Mircea Eliade, 6:530–1. New York: Macmillan, 1987.

Doty, William G. *Mythography: The Study of Myths and Rituals.* Tuscaloosa: University of Alabama Press, 1986. Revised Second Edition, 2000.

Dumezil, Georges. *Archaic Roman Religion.* Trans. Philip Krapp. Chicago: University of Chicago Press, 1970.

————. *L'ideologie tripartie des Indo-Européens.* Brussels: Latomus 1958.

Eliade, Mircea, ed. *The Encyclopedia of Religion.* 16 vols. New York: Macmillan, 1987.

————. *Patterns in Comparative Religion* (1958). Cleveland: Meridian, 1963.

Ellis, Peter Berresford. *Dictionary of Celtic Mythology.* New York: Oxford University Press, 1992.

Fee, Christopher with David Leeming. *Gods, Heroes, and Kings: The Battle for Mythic Britain.* New York: Oxford University Press, 2001.

Foster, B. O., trans. *Livy: History of Rome.* Cambridge, Mass: Harvard, 1988.

Frazer, Sir James G. *The Golden Bough* (1923). London: Macmillan, 1971.

————. *The New Golden Bough.* Ed. Theodor H. Gaster. New York: Mentor, 1964.

Freud, Sigmund. *Totem and Taboo.* Trans. A. A. Brill. New York: Moffat, Yard, 1918.

Frey-Rohn, Liliane. *From Freud to Jung: A Comparative Study of the Psychology of the Unconscious.* Trans. Fred and Evelyn Engree. New York: G. P. Putnam's Sons, 1974.

Gaster, Theodor H. "Heroes." In *The Encyclopedia of Religion*, ed. Mircea Eliade, 6:302–5. New York: Macmillan, 1987.

Gimbutas, Marija. *The Goddesses and Gods of Old Europe: Myths and Cult Images.* Rev. ed. Berkeley: University of California Press, 1982.

———. *The Language of the Goddess.* San Francisco: HarperCollins, 1989.

———. "Prehistoric Religions: Old Europe" and "Megalithic Religion." In *The Encyclopedia of Religion*, ed. Mircea Eliade, 11:506–15; 9:336–44. New York: Macmillan, 1987.

———. "Slavic Religion." In *The Encyclopedia of Religion*, ed. Mircea Eliade, 13:353–61. New York: Macmillan, 1987.

Graves, Robert. *The Greek Myths.* 2 vols. London and New York: Penguin, 1970.

Gray, Elizabeth A. *Cath Maige Tuired: The Second Battle of Mag Tuired.* London: Irish Texts Society, 1982.

Green, Miranda. *Celtic Myths.* The Legendary Past Series. London: British Museum Press, 1993.

Grimal, Pierre, ed. *Larousse World Mythology.* London and New York: Hamlyn, 1974.

Hadas, Moses, ed. *Complete Works of Tacetus.* New York: McGraw Hill, 1964.

Hammonds, Carolyn, trans. Julius Caesar, *The Seven Commentaries on the Gallic War.* New York: Oxford, 1998.

Harakas, Stanley Samuel. "Christianity in Eastern Europe." In *The Encyclopedia of Religion*, ed. Mircea Eliade, 3:372–9. New York: Macmillan, 1987.

Harrison, Jane. *Epilegomena to the Study of Greek Religion and Themis: A Study of the Social Origins of Greek Religion.* Hyde Park, N.Y.: University Books, 1962.

Hesiod. *Theogony.* Trans. Norman O. Brown. Indianapolis: Bobbs-Merrill, 1953.

Hollander, Lee M., trans. *The Poetic Edda* (by Snorri Sturluson). Austin: University of Texas Press, 1962.

Homer. *Iliad.* Trans. Richard Lattimore. Chicago: Phoenix Books, 1961.

———. *The Odyssey of Homer.* Trans. Robert Fitzgerald. Garden City, N.Y.: Doubleday, 1963.

Honko, Lauri. "Finno-Ugric Religions: An Overview." In *The Encyclopedia of Religion*, ed. Mircea Eliade, 5:335. New York: Macmillan, 1987.

Jackson, Guida M. *Encyclopedia of Traditional Epics.* Santa Barbara, Calif.: ABC-CLIO, 1994.

Jones, Gwyn. *A History of the Vikings.* Rev. ed. Oxford: Oxford University Press, 1984.

——— and Thomas Jones, trans. *The Mabinogion.* New rev. ed. Everyman Library. Rutland, Vt.: Charles E. Tuttle Co., 1993.

Jung, Carl Gustav. *The Archetypes and the Collective Unconscious* (1934, 1954). Princeton: Princeton University Press, 1959.

Kerenyi, C. *The Gods of the Greeks*. London: Thames and Hudson, 1951.

————. *The Heroes of the Greeks*. New York: Grove Press, 1960.

Kinsella, Thomas, trans. *The Tain*. Oxford: Oxford University Press, 1970.

Larrington, Carolyne, ed. *The Feminist Companion to Mythology*. London: Pandora, 1992.

Leeming, David. *A Dictionary of Asian Mythology*. New York: Oxford University Press, 2001.

————. *Myth: A Biography of Belief*. New York: Oxford University Press, 2002.

————. "Quests." In *The Encyclopedia of Religion*, ed. Mircea Eliade, 12:146–52. New York: Macmillan, 1987.

————. *Mythology: The Voyage of the Hero*. New York: Oxford University Press, 1998.

————. *The World of Myth*. New York: Oxford University Press, 1990.

———— and Jake Page. *God: Myths of the Male Divine*. New York: Oxford University Press, 1996.

———— and Jake Page. *Goddess: Myths of the Female Divine*. New York: Oxford University Press, 1994.

———— and Jake Page. *Myths, Legends, and Folktales of America*. New York: Oxford University Press, 1999.

———— and Jake Page. *The Mythology of Native North America*. Norman: University of Oklahoma Press, 1998.

———— with Margaret Leeming. *A Dictionary of Creation Myths*. New York: Oxford University Press, 1994.

Lévi-Strauss, Claude. *Myth and Meaning*. New York: Harper & Row, 1979.

————. *The Raw and the Cooked*. Trans. John and Doreen Weightman. New York: Harper & Row, 1969.

Lincoln, Bruce. "Indo-European Religions." In *The Encyclopedia of Religion*, ed. Mircea Eliade, 7:198–204. New York: Macmillan, 1987.

Livy. See Foster.

Lovelock, James E. *Gaia: A New Look at Life on Earth*. New York and Oxford: Oxford University Press, 1979.

MacAlister, R.A.S. *Lebor Gabala Erenn* (Book of Invasions). 5 volumes. Dublin: Irish Text Society, 1956.

MacCana, Proinsias. *Celtic Mythology*. London: Hamlyn, 1970.

————. "Celtic Religion." In *The Encyclopedia of Religion*, ed, Mircea Eliade, 3:148–66. New York: Macmillan, 1987.

McLean, Adam. *The Triple Goddess: An Exploration of the Archetypal Feminine*. Grand Rapids, Mich.: Phanes Press, 1989.

Mallory, J. P. *In Search of the Indo-Europeans: Language, Archaeology and Myth*. London: Thames and Hudson, 1989.

Momigliano, Arnaldo. "Roman Religion: The Imperial Period." In *The Encyclopedia of Religion*, ed. Mircea Eliade, 12:462–71. New York: Macmillan, 1987.

Morford, Mark P. O., and Robert J. Lenardon, eds. *Classical Mythology*. New York and London: Longman, 1985.

Murray, Gilbert. *Five Stages of Greek Religion* (1951). Garden City, N.Y.: Doubleday, 1955.

Narr, Karl J. "Paleolithic Religion," trans. Matthew J. O'Connell. In *The Encyclopedia of Religion*, ed. Mircea Eliade, 11:14959. New York: Macmillan, 1987.

Nilsson, Martin. *A History of Greek Religion*. Trans. F. J. Fielden. New York: W. W. Norton, 1965.

———. *The Mycenaean Origin of Greek Mythology* (1932). New York: W. W. Norton, 1963.

O'Flaherty, Wendy Doniger. *Hindu Myths: A Sourcebook Translated from the Sanskrit*. Harmondsworth, U.K.: Penguin, 1975.

Otto, Walter F. *The Homeric Gods: The Spiritual Significance of Greek Religion*. London: Thames and Hudson, 1954.

Ovid. *Ovid's Metamorphoses*. Trans. Charles Boer. Dallas, Tex.: Spring Publications, 1989.

Oxford Study Bible. Ed. M. Jack Suggs, et al. New York: Oxford University Press, 1992.

Page, R. I. *Norse Myths*. The Legendary Past Series. London: British Museum Press, 1990.

Panikkar, Raimundo. "Deity." In *The Encyclopedia of Religion*, ed. Mircea Eliade, 4:264–76. New York: Macmillan, 1987.

Pelon, Olivier. "Aegean Religions," trans. Anne Marzin. In *The Encyclopedia of Religion*, ed. Mircea Eliade, 1:32–39. New York: Macmillan, 1987.

Pelikan, Jaroslav. " Christianity: An Overview" and "Christianity in Western Europe." In *The Encyclopedia of Religion*, ed. Mircea Eliade, 3:348–62; 379–87. New York: Macmillan, 1987.

Plato. *The Republic*, trans. Desmond Lee. New York: Penguin, 1976.

Polome, Edgar C. "Germanic Religion." In *The Encyclopedia of Religion*, ed. Mircea Eliade, 5:520–36. New York: Macmillan, 1987.

Puhvel, Jaan. *Comparative Mythology*. Baltimore: Johns Hopkins University Press, 1987.

Raglan, Lord Fitzroy. *The Hero: A Study in Tradition, Myth, and Drama* (1937). New York: Vintage, 1956.

Rank, Otto. *The Myth of the Birth of the Hero and Other Writings*. New York: Vintage, 1959.

Rees, Alwyn, and Brinley Rees. *Celtic Heritage: Ancient Tradition in Ireland and Wales*. London: Thames and Hudson, 1961.

Rosenberg, Donna. *World Mythology: An Anthology of the Great Myths and Epics*. Lincolnwood, Ill.: National Textbook, 1986.

Rudd, Niall, and Jonathan Powell, ed. and trans. *The Republic & the Law by Cicero.* New York: Oxford, 1998.

Saxo Grammaticus, see Davidson and Fisher.

Schilling, Robert. "Roman Religion: The Early Period," trans. Paul C. Duggan. In *The Encyclopedia of Religion,* ed. Mircea Eliade, 12:445–61. New York: Macmillan, 1987.

Siikala, Anna-Leena. "Finnic Religions," trans. Susan Sinisalo. In *The Encyclopedia of Religion,* ed. Mircea Eliade, 5:323–30. New York: Macmillan, 1897.

Smith, Adam. *The Wealth of Nations.* New York: Random House, 1977.

Sproul, Barbara. *Primal Myths: Creation Myths Around the World.* New York: HarperCollins, 1991.

Srejovic, Dragoslav. "Neolithic Religion," trans. Veselin Kostic. In *The Encyclopedia of Religion,* ed. Mircea Eliade, 10:352–60. New York: Macmillan, 1987.

Sturluson, Snorri. See Hollander; see Young.

Tacitus. See Hadas.

Terry, Patricia, trans. *Poems of the Vikings: The Elder Edda.* Indianapolis: Bobbs-Merrill, 1982.

Turville-Petre, E.O.G. *Myth and Religion in the North.* New York: Holt, Rinehart & Winston, 1964.

van Buitenan, J.A.B, trans. *The Mahābhārata.* Chicago: University of Chicago Press, 1973–1978.

Vergil, *Aeneid,* trans. Robert Fitzgerald. New York: Vintage, 1990.

Vernant, Jean-Pierre. "Greek Religion," trans. Anne Marzin. In *The Encyclopedia of Religion,* ed. Mircea Eliade, 6:99–118. New York: Macmillan, 1987.

Walker, Barbara C. *The Woman's Encyclopedia of Myths and Secrets.* San Francisco: Harper & Row, 1983.

Watts, Alan. *Myth and Ritual in Christianity.* Boston: Beacon Press, 1968.

Weston, Jessie L. *From Ritual to Romance: An Account of the Holy Grail from Ancient Ritual to Christian Symbol.* Garden City, N.Y.: Doubleday, 1957.

White, Lynn, Jr. "Christian Myth and Christian History." In *Machina ex Deo: Essays in the Dynamism of Western Culture.* Cambridge, Mass.: MIT Press, 1969.

Young, Jean I., trans. *The Prose Edda of Snorri Sturluson: Tales from Norse Mythology.* Berkeley: University of California Press, 1954.

Index